LI

b
ne

FIN
OI

Plea
Off
(Tel
has

RES
bo
re

A

THEMES
& VARIATIONS

By the same Author

*

Novels

APE AND ESSENCE
TIME MUST HAVE A STOP
AFTER MANY A SUMMER
EYELESS IN GAZA
BRAVE NEW WORLD
POINT COUNTER POINT
THOSE BARREN LEAVES
ANTIC HAY
CROME YELLOW

Biography

GREY EMINENCE

Short Stories

BRIEF CANDLES
TWO OR THREE GRACES
LITTLE MEXICAN
MORTAL COILS
LIMBO

Essays and Belles Lettres

THE PERENNIAL PHILOSOPHY
SCIENCE, LIBERTY AND PEACE
THE ART OF SEEING
ENDS AND MEANS
MUSIC AT NIGHT
VULGARITY IN LITERATURE
DO WHAT YOU WILL
PROPER STUDIES
JESTING PILATE
ALONG THE ROAD
ON THE MARGIN
TEXT AND PRETEXTS
BEYOND THE MEXIQUE BAY
THE OLIVE TREE

Poetry

THE CICADAS
LEDA

Drama

THE GIOCONDA SMILE
THE WORLD OF LIGHT

Chatto & Windus

THEMES
And Variations

ALDOUS HUXLEY

CHATTO & WINDUS

1950

PUBLISHED BY
Chatto and Windus
LONDON
*
Clarke, Irwin & Co. Ltd
TORONTO

CONTENTS

* *Printed in* Horizon *under the title of 'Death and the Baroque'*

ILLUSTRATIONS

VARIATIONS ON A PHILOSOPHER

I

Portrait of a Philosopher

THAT summer of 1816 the Quaestor of the Chamber of Deputies was taking a cure at a small but fashionable spa in the Pyrenees. On the morning of July 30th he was called, as usual, at six o'clock and, as usual, experienced that awful sense of emptiness, confusion and incapacity which now made his daily resurrection from sleep an event to be dreaded. For the first hour after getting out of bed and for much more than the first hour after rising from table, he knew the humiliation of being less than himself, of undergoing in his own person the triumph of the animal over the human, of physiology over intellect and will. "Wretched man that I am," he kept repeating as he put on his clothes, "who will deliver me from the body of this death?" *De corpore mortis hujus.* Who will deliver me, who will deliver me? There was no answer.

He left the house. The morning was cold, with menacing clouds and a wind that seemed to blow through him. His nerves responded, like an Aeolian harp, with the most excruciating discord. It was going, he foresaw, to be one of his bad days.

The Quaestor turned into the bathing establishment, was shown into his cubicle and a few minutes later stretched himself out voluptuously in the warm mineralized water.

Through the steam of sulphuretted hydrogen an attendant appeared, bringing half a bottle of Cauterets water and an equal quantity of ass's milk. The Quaestor mixed the two together, drank, dried his hands and opened his copy of Pascal's *Pensées*, with notes by Voltaire and Condorcet. It was to these notes at the end of the volume that he first turned. Not in the hope of any profit or enlightenment, but simply because, by their shallowness, their deliberately frivolous incomprehension, they filled him with such indignation. He read and re-read them as a man perversely touches his aching tooth, merely for the sake of feeling a renewal of his pain. Here was Voltaire on contemplation. Thinking it "very droll that anyone should imagine that laziness was a title to greatness and action a lowering and diminution of our nature." Idiot, fool! But, after all, why should one expect such a creature to understand the true nature of contemplation? But enough of this commentary of apes! The Quaestor turned back the pages until he found himself among the *Pensées*.

"We are not satisfied," he read, "with the life we have in ourselves and our own being; we want to live an imaginary life in other people's idea of us. Hence all our efforts are directed to seeming what we are not. We labour incessantly to preserve and embellish this imaginary being, and neglect that which is really ours."

The Quaestor put down the book, took another gulp of milk and Epsom salts and ruefully reflected that all his own troubles had arisen from this desire to seem what in fact he was not. To seem a man of action, when in fact he was a contemplative; to seem a politician, when nature had made him an introspective psychologist; to seem a wit, when God had intended him for a sage. What folly! And there were other follies even more discreditable. He looked down through the water at his withered shanks and scrawny body. How ridiculous, how lamentably unheroic! He was almost fifty and prematurely old. *Ecce enim breves anni transeunt et semitam, per quam non revertar, ambulo.* And yet with pomatum and toilet waters, with cream of almonds and powder, he still made efforts to seem young, to look like the sort of man that young persons of the sex would find as attractive as he still found them. To what end did he thus make a fool of himself? With what intentions? His timidity and his moral principles were such that he would never act upon these vague desires of his. And he was clear-sighted enough to be aware that the young persons looked upon him as an old bore with one foot in the grave. And yet he persisted in this effort to seem other than himself. His folly was gratuitous. He pursued it and persisted in it as he ought to be pursuing and persisting in virtue—for its own sake and as its own reward.

But, oh, the musk and the patchouli! And, under the chandeliers, those arms and throats, those high-busked bosoms offered as though on platters—on silver salvers, like the strawberry ices at the reception given last month by the Keeper of the Seals. How graciously his host had addressed him, how attentively he had listened, while the Quaestor expressed his views on the best way to serve the Dynasty! And then, as usual, had come the moment of humiliation. In the middle of a sentence he was suddenly aware that the great man had moved away and was talking to M. de Chateaubriand—M. de Chateaubriand, around whom at that moment three pairs of naked arms, three bosoms on platters, three flawless necks, three flushed and animated faces were grouped in attitudes of almost reverential admiration. These geniuses, these golden voices united to pinchbeck minds! Bitterly the Quaestor reminded himself of what he had so frequently observed in the course of his far from brilliant career—that success in public life is due more often to a man's defects than to his merits. He sighed, drank some more milk and purgative, then lay back and closed his eyes. His mind wandered. When the attendant knocked at the door and announced that it was eight o'clock, he realized with a start that he had wasted yet another of the few thousands of hours—or perhaps only a few hundreds, a few scores—which were now left to him. *Miserere nobis!* With an inward groan he got out of the bath and, feeling if anything rather worse for his medication, started to dry the bag of bones which had once been the graceful body of one of Louis XVI's youngest guardsmen.

He dressed, hurried back to his lodgings, undressed again, went to bed for an hour, but was unable to relax, dressed for the third time and sat down, agitated and thoroughly out of sorts, to his correspondence. His wife came in with his coffee. How was he feeling? Not well at all. Was there anything she could do? No, he snapped, and was immediately ashamed of himself, but at the same time resentfully wished she would leave him alone. Pointedly he reached for his pen and started to write. She took the hint and went out. Poor woman, he thought, as he heard the door close behind her; but all the same, thank God!

Laboriously, against enormous internal obstacles, he wrote a report to the Minister of the Interior on the state of public opinion in his constituency; then took a fresh sheet of paper and began to jot down those notes on Kant for which his friend Stapfer had asked him.

"That celebrated philosopher," he wrote, "mistakenly drew a line between the principles of cognition and those of human morality. He failed to see that the primitive act of willing is at one and the same time the principle of knowledge and the principle of human morality. Without the intimate sense of effort which constitutes the 'I,' there can be nothing in the understanding, and thus even the ideas of sensation and perception are dependent upon willing. As for the noumenal self . . ." His right eyelid began to twitch. It was the last straw. He rang the bell and gave orders for his horse to be saddled. What happened next was recorded that evening in his *Journal*.

"The state of my nerves was bad, and I was just mounting my horse in the hope that a brisk canter would put my sorry machine to rights, when the Duchesse de Rohan, accompanied by my colleague Castel-Bajac, knocked at my door to take up a collection for the poor of Saint-Sauveur. I knew that this collection was to be made, and I had decided in advance to give six francs, thinking that this would be the accepted rate for visitors in comfortable circumstances. Accordingly I dropped my crown into the collecting bag, wondering, with a certain embarrassment, whether I was doing the right thing. That I had not done the right thing was made very plain, when the Duchess mentioned the names of several persons who had given her one or two louis. Her words overwhelmed me, and I immediately experienced an agitation and a sense of remorse that could not have been more intense if I had committed the basest and most dishonourable of acts. But I lacked the presence of mind to speak and allowed the charitable lady to take her departure without uttering a word.

"From that moment it was impossible for me to think of anything else. What would the Duchess think of me? What would be the comments of my colleague, whose feelings towards the Quaestor of the Chamber were anything but friendly? Would I not be made the laughing-stock of the whole company? And my offering, so disproportionate to my disposition—would it not be treated as a symptom of the most sordid avarice? . . . I, who, in most circumstances, care so little for money—how simple it would have been for me to give the Duchess a louis! Why had I not opened my purse and shown my willingness to come to the aid of the unfortunate—merely remarking, which is all too true, that a collection taken up in this way for a multitude of the poor can be but of the smallest assistance to each one in particular?

"Instead of this, what awkwardness in my behaviour towards the Duchess! What downright bad manners! I was inconsolable. . . .

"I mounted my horse, hoping to divert myself from an idea so wearisome in its fixity. But it pursued me wherever I went. I cut short my ride and returned home with the intention of seeking out the Duchess and adding a louis to my contribution, with a graceful little explanation.

"With this in mind I went and walked up and down in front of her house, but did not go in for fear of making a fool of myself yet again. I went home to dinner full of the same anxiety. My fixed idea haunted me to the point of making me talk and gesticulate to myself. I caught myself several times in this condition bordering almost on insanity.

"During dinner I said nothing to my wife; for I was absorbed in my own thoughts, and anyhow I never confide to others my feelings or impressions when they are sad or painful."

It was to his Diary and not to his wife that the Quaestor confided his troubles. He himself remained unconsoled, but posterity has been the gainer. The profit was not his, it is all ours—for the *Journal Intime* of Maine de Biran has emerged, after all these years, as one of the classics of the inner life, a book to be read and ruminated and read again.

Philosophy is written for the most part in terms of the highest abstractions, the widest generalizations. Rightly, I suppose, and properly. Nevertheless, it seems good, for a change, to consider some of its problems, not, so to speak, in the void, but within the framework of an actual existence. And if that existence should be that of a man who was himself a philosopher, so much the better. For in that case we shall be in a position to think our thoughts in relation, not only to a particular life in time, but also to the system of ideas in terms of which the proprietor of that life sought to interpret his experience.

Maine de Biran's *Journal Intime* is a document almost unique in the history of philosophy. Thanks to its minute and detailed sincerity, we know Biran as we know no other of the great metaphysicians of the past. We know how he felt from day to day and what he thought about his feelings; we know how his bodily states affected his mind, and his mental states, his body; we know how he reacted to nature, to works of art, to persons of various temperaments, abilities and social conditions; we know what he wished and willed, and what he actually accomplished; we know what he thought and we know the psychological and even the physiological context of his thinking, what and how he actually *was* while playing the part of a philosopher. For all these reasons and because he was a man of the highest ability (his philosophical contemporaries called him 'the master of us all' and 'the greatest French metaphysician since Malebranche'), Biran provides us with a particularly helpful frame of reference within which to do our own thinking about the perennial problem of philosophy. In what follows I shall make no attempt to write a new biography of Maine de Biran or to offer yet another critique of his system. My concern is with certain aspects of man's nature and destiny; and my purpose is to discuss these matters in the light, now revealingly bright, now no less revealingly dim, of Maine de Biran's life and writings. Let us begin with a brief record of the external facts.

François-Pierre Gontier de Biran, later known (after the inheritance of an estate called Maine) as François-Pierre Maine de Biran, was born on November 29th, 1766, at the capital city of the old province of Périgord, where his family, notable without being actually noble, had for three centuries played an important part in local society and local politics. His grandfather had been Mayor of Bergerac, and so had his great-grandfather. His father practised as a physician in the same town and managed the family estates in its vicinity. Educated at home and later at the College of the Doctrinaires at Périgueux, young Biran received a sound eighteenth-century grounding in Latin, Greek and mathematics. At eighteen he entered the Royal Bodyguard and became a young man about town and the court. "What the world calls pleasure" (and it was the world, let us remember, of Choderlos de Laclos and Andréa de Nerciat) "I tasted to the full." He tasted it for five years. Then came 1789. In October of that year Biran saw action, fighting with the Compagnie de Noailles to defend Versailles against the Parisian mob. The Revolution took its course, and a little later the Royal Bodyguard was disbanded. Hoping to start his military career anew in the Engineers, Biran plunged into the study of mathematics and the physical sciences. But as time went on it became clear that an ex-guardsman's chances of getting into the new army were growing steadily smaller, his chances of going to prison and perhaps the scaffold steadily greater. In 1793 young Biran prudently decided to go home to Périgord. During his absence in Paris both his parents had died and he now found himself the proprietor of an estate, with a small but regular income and, to live in, a seventeenth-century manor house five miles from Bergerac. The name of this house was Grateloup, from *gratum lupis*, 'agreeable to wolves,' and in this sylvan solitude he took refuge from a world of revolutionary violence. Outside, beyond the sheltering wall of trees, the indefatigable Lakanal was riding through the country, organizing groups of 'civic apostles,' whose duty it was to preach the revolutionary gospel to the peasants and to collect gossip about suspected royalists. Thanks to these apostles, six members of the Biran clan were briefly imprisoned, four went into voluntary exile. Our philosopher, however, was left in peace.

After the fall of Robespierre the government purged its civil service of all extreme Jacobins and appointed men of less radical opinions to fill the vacancies. Biran came from a family which enjoyed a high reputation for probity and efficiency in the public service. In the summer of 1795 he was appointed Administrator of the department of the Dordogne. That same year he fell in love with, and married, Marie-Louise Fournier, the young widow of one of his cousins, M. du Cluzeau, who had gone abroad during the Terror and, never having been heard of since, was presumed to have died.

After two years as Administrator of his native province Biran was elected by his fellow citizens as their representative of the Council of Five Hundred. The young deputy's politics were frankly anti-revolutionary—so much so that, before he could take his seat, his election was declared invalid. Biran found himself simultaneously out of a job and out of politics. Relieved rather than distressed, he plunged into philosophy and the joys of domesticity. Those years at Grateloup, with his wife and young children, among his books and papers, were the happiest of his life—so happy, indeed, that he kept no record of them. While Marie-Louise was alive he never opened his Diary.

It was during this period that Biran first attracted notice as a philosopher. From the Institute of France he received an honourable mention for his first *Memoir on Habit*, a gold medal for the second, augmented and revised version of the same treatise. Prizes crowned the works submitted to the Academies of Berlin and Copenhagen. He became the friend and correspondent of such representatives of the older school of thought as Cabanis and Destutt de Tracy, as well as of younger men, such as de Gérando and Royer-Collard.

Then, in 1805, after only eight years of marriage, Marie-Louise suddenly died. According to La Valette-Monbrun,

Biran's latest biographer, who had the information from a direct descendant of the philosopher, her last illness was brought on by a painful emotional shock. Du Cluzeau, her first husband, was not dead, as had been assumed; he had merely been a poor correspondent. One fine day, after eleven years of foreign wanderings, he calmly walked into Marie-Louise's drawing-room at Bergerac. Three weeks later she was dead. Biran's unhappiness was extreme. Grief deprived him of all power to think or act, even of all desire to live. But in the end time, necessity and habit saved him in spite of himself. After six months of mental and physical prostration Biran gradually re-emerged into life. He embarked again on his reading, his fragmentary composition, his analytical meditations. He wrote long letters to his philosophical friends and followed up the letters by personal visits.

This was the period of his intimacy with the Ideologists of Auteuil, Cabanis and Destutt de Tracy. "The two friends," he wrote, "lived solely for their beloved Ideology. Ideology, they say, must change the whole face of the world, and that precisely is why those who, for their own good reasons, would like the world to go on being stupid" (the reference is, of course, to the First Consul) "detest Ideologists and Ideology." Biran was too much of a realist, too close to the facts of inner experience, to accept a system which owed its specious perfection to the crudest kind of over-simplification. The sages of Auteuil hopefully regarded him as their disciple; but in fact, as they were later forced to admit, they had incubated a bird of quite another species.

Two years after his wife's death, Biran was back again in harness, this time as Counsellor to the Prefect of Périgueux. It was a very modest post; but he needed the money and had been unable to find anything better. He would have preferred a professorship of mathematics, or a rectorate in the University. No suitable posts were available. Well, then, if he had to re-enter the administration, what about a prefecture? His friends, Malleville and de Gérando, did their best for him; but without success. Malleville even presented the Third Consul with a handsomely bound copy of the *Memoir on Habit*; the effect was decisive and disastrous. After skimming through the book, Lebrun gravely remarked that "the man who could write such a work will never be good for anything." He was, of course, perfectly right. The *Memoir on Habit* is a masterpiece of analytical introspection and, in a man of affairs, a gift for analytical introspection is not merely useless, but may even be an actual handicap. The Consulate gave place to the Empire; but the official opinion of our philosopher's political abilities did not change. Biran had to be content with his Counsellorship. A year passed and the Emperor relented a little. The Counsellor was promoted to be Sub-Prefect of Bergerac.

Zeal was the order of the day and, during the six years of his reign at Bergerac, Biran was admirably zealous. Few of the local peasants could read or write or speak anything but a barbarous patois; but the Sub-Prefect issued innumerable and emphatically eloquent proclamations, exhorting them to be thankful that the Revolution was over and to express their gratitude to the Emperor by joining the National Guard and, above all, by paying their taxes—those crushing war-time taxes which it was so horribly distasteful to have to collect by threats or naked force. In the intervals he built roads and bridges, preached afforestation and modern methods in agriculture, set up centres for the gratuitous vaccination of the poor. Distressed by the fact that people were constantly falling into the Dordogne, he installed in the hospital the latest marvel of the scientific age, a *machine fumigatoire*, guaranteed by its inventor to restore life to the drowned. He founded a Medical Society, brought back the Sisters of Charity, reformed the local secondary school and imported from Switzerland a pupil of Pestalozzi's to direct an institution for younger children. In 1809 his compatriots did what they had done fourteen years before and elected him as their representative to the Legislative Assembly. But a Sub-Prefect might not resign until his successor had been appointed; and since the Emperor chose to wait three years before making the nomination, Biran did not take his seat until 1812. From that date until his death in 1824 he was to serve as deputy for Bergerac, spending the greater part of each year in Paris, while his second wife, whom he married in 1814, stayed at home and managed the estate. Under Napoleon and, later, the Bourbons, a deputy received a salary which was sufficient, in Biran's case, to make all the difference between a pinched, rather shabby gentility and easy independence. He could now buy all the books he wanted, entertain his scientific and philosophical friends to dinner, take cabs and indulge a propensity for lending money to all who asked for it.

Biran entered public life just as Napoleon was about to leave it. As a functionary of the State, he had served the Emperor well and faithfully. As an anti-revolutionary, he was thankful to Bonaparte for having restored internal order. But as a child of the Enlightenment, he loathed the military dictator and his horde of soldiers; as a royalist by conviction and sentiment, he abhorred the usurper of an authority which belonged by right to the sons of St. Louis. At the end of 1813 Biran had an opportunity for giving public expression to his feelings about the Emperor. With his friend Laîné and the three other members of the Commission of Five, he drew up a resolution, later adopted by the Chamber, demanding an immediate end to hostilities, the conclusion of a just peace and a greater measure of liberty for the French people. Napoleon's reply was to dissolve the Chamber and continue a hopeless war to its inevitable conclusion.

When the Bourbons returned in 1814, Biran found himself almost a hero and was rewarded by being made Quaestor of the Chamber with twice the ordinary deputy's salary. The Hundred Days sent him back to Grateloup, the Second Restoration confirmed his Quaestorship. Prevented by shyness and the weakness of his voice from being a successful orator, he did all his parliamentary work behind the scenes, on committees or in private conversations with the ministers and his more influential colleagues. A convinced moderate, he was at home in no party, being disliked by the Ultras as no better than a Liberal, by the Liberals as a reactionary monarchist. It was an uncomfortable position; but fortunately Biran had other interests than those of politics. After consulting his conscience he decided that he was not in duty bound to give more than six hours a day to his parliamentary functions. The rest of his time might legitimately be devoted to philosophy and the occupations of private life. He was on intimate terms with some of the most eminent men of his age—Ampère, Cuvier, Guizot, Victor Cousin,

Royer-Collard, de Gérando. Over the dinner-table, or walking in the Luxembourg, or at the fortnightly meetings of the Metaphysical Society, he discussed with them the problems of man's nature and position in the universe. And meanwhile he was for ever writing and deleting and re-writing some part of the comprehensive treatise in which he hoped some day to set forth his completed system.

When he died, this *magnum opus* was still an unrealized dream. Given the nature of Biran's mind, it could not have been otherwise. An empiricist of the spirit, he was always ready to modify his opinions in the light of new experience. His thought never completely crystallized into a system, but remained, in regard to certain vital subjects, tentative and, as it were, fluid to the very end of his life. That end came in 1824. His fellow philosophers paid their tribute of respect and regret; the electors of Bergerac chose another deputy, and his son Felix was heard to say that he wished the old man had left fewer books and papers and more government securities.

"O why was I born with a different face?" It was a question that, in the course of his daily soliloquies, rose over and over again to Biran's lips. He was painfully aware that he had not been "born like the rest of his race," that he was a foreigner, far from home in an environment he did not like and with which he was congenitally unfitted to deal. But whereas the poet's unlikeness to his fellows was due to an excess of imagination and intuition, the philosopher belonged to that more numerous class of aliens, the temperamental introverts. A portrait of Biran at twenty-nine reveals one of those slender, small-boned, thin-muscled persons, in whom the nerves and vital organs are uncomfortably close to the surface. Such persons are as a rule sensitive to excess and have a tendency, in mere self-protection, to turn inwards, away from their surroundings, which they experience as a standing menace to their well-being. Like the world of all extreme cerebrotonics, Biran's universe was primarily that of his own inner experiences and only secondarily that of other people and autonomous objects. He knew that, whereas he was an alien, most men were more or less at home in the world and that some had an all but infallible instinct for finding their way through life. To make up for his own lack of this instinct, he was gifted (as most of his fellows were not) with "a rapid tact in regard to what is going on within me." In his own eyes it was this tact which, above all else, qualified him to be a psychologist and a metaphysician.

An extreme cerebrotonic can never be a successful behaviourist and, conversely, an extreme somatotonic or extreme viscerotonic is organically debarred from the psychology of introspection. By nature Biran was quite incapable of behaviourism, and this incapacity was, by systematic exercise, converted into a state almost of solipsistic preoccupation with the inner life. His *Journal Intime* is consistently intimate; it contains no anecdotes, no descriptions of other people, no speculations as to their motives, their modes of thought, or the reasons for their idiosyncrasies. Biran had an opportunity to meet almost 'everybody who was anybody' and was, as we have seen, on intimate terms with some of the most remarkable men and women of his day. The Diary merely records their names; of their appearance, their behaviour, their character, our philosopher says nothing. He dines with Mme. de Staël, he meets Chateaubriand; but what he thought and felt about those rather alarming forces of nature disguised as human beings, or whether indeed he thought and felt anything about them as they were in themselves, we do not know. He merely states that he saw them and proceeds, if the meeting took place on one of his good days, to describe his own euphoria, if on one of his bad days, to analyse the psycho-physiological causes of his melancholy or his sense of frustrated inadequacy. Foreign celebrities possess as little autonomous reality as his compatriots. Wellington and Brougham are no more than names in a list of those present, and when he dines out to meet Maria Edgeworth, all he says is that he "permitted himself to be carried away by disordered movements"—movements which, we can be sure, had their source, not in the lady's charms, which in 1820 can hardly have been overpowering, but in the state of the philosopher's nervous system. In the six or seven hundred pages of Biran's *Journal* I have found but one comment on another human being as existing independently of the diarist, in his own right. Speaking of Destutt de Tracy, Biran says that "he is, in spite of his caustic tongue, a kindly and lovable man. He has had the misfortune to lose his sight, and supports this affliction with courage." That is all. And of his other philosopher friends—of such persons as Ampère, the ingenuous eccentric and many-sided man of genius, as Cuvier, the founder of a science, as Guizot, the scholar who was one day to control the destinies of France—he says nothing at all. They exist in the Diary only in so far as they react, favourably or unfavourably, to Biran's psychological and metaphysical views.

How significant, in this context, is the description of our philosopher given, many years after his death, by an old lady who had known him when she was a young girl and he, the Sub-Prefect of Bergerac! The young girl was the daughter of M. Maurice, the Prefect of Périgueux. Not infrequently the Sub-Prefect rode over to dine with his official superior and unofficial friend. On these occasions general conversation tended to dwindle into philosophical argument. More than half a century later, Mlle. Maurice recalled that "the ego (*le moi*) played an important part in these discussions. My sister and I have not forgotten that, at every enunciation of this monosyllable, M. de Biran would energetically press the tips of his extended and unseparated fingers against his chest, in order, no doubt, more emphatically to assert the fact of his personality."

Too much the introvert to be concerned with other people's unconscious behaviour, Biran himself would never have noticed such a fact as this, or at least would never have troubled to record it. In this respect the Maurice girls were better psychologists than he. Intuitively they recognized that there was something profoundly significant in the Sub-Prefect's curious gesture. *Le moi*, and he points at himself; *le moi*, and again the rigid fingers turn back towards the heart. It happens invariably, it happens automatically. Habitual gestures of this kind are not very common; but one may observe them frequently enough to be sure that they are always a symptom of an intense self-consciousness. This self-consciousness is sometimes unresistingly egotistic; sometimes, as in Biran's case, it is associated with a constant preoccupation with moral problems, an unremitting effort to conform to a high ideal. The ego can be intensely aware of itself either as deliberate and sophisticated Epicurean, as earnest and virtuous Stoic, or as ruthless power-lover. As twice-born Christian, twice-born Buddhist or Vedantist, it ceases to be a self-conscious ego, and becomes "not I, but Christ, Mind, Atman in me."

Human beings are not all of one kind, but vary continuously between the viable extremes of a tri-polar system. Any individual is a mixture, in varying proportions, of three physical and closely correlated pyschological components. The exclusively introspective psychologist has it in his power to discover the characteristics which are common to all human beings, together with those peculiar to himself and to all the other individuals, who stand in the same relation as he does to the three co-ordinates of the classificatory system. Of the traits which distinguish men and women standing in a different relation to the three co-ordinates, he cannot, merely by looking into himself, discover anything at all. To acquire this kind of extensive knowledge of psychology, he must learn the, to him, rather difficult art of looking outwards.

Conversely the born outward-lookers must, if they are to have an intensive knowledge of the human soul, learn how to examine and dissect their own. Introspective methods require to be supplemented by those of behaviourism; behaviouristic methods by those of introspection. Biran, as we have seen, made no effort to overcome his native incapacity for outwardness. The results were what might have been expected. "In the practical affairs of life," he sadly remarks, "my psychological knowledge does not help me at all." And how touching is the innocence, the *naïveté* even, which has its source in our introvert's often abysmal ignorance of the external world! He is over fifty when, in a Duchess's drawing-room, he first makes the startling discovery that "there is a natural affinity between persons of the same caste." At about the same time he is not only shocked, but actually astonished, when he learns that the Minister of Police under the legitimate monarch is using methods of corruptive persuasion identical with those employed by his predecessor under Napoleon. And a year or two later he is equally surprised and still more deeply shocked to discover that a lady, with whom he was in the habit of discussing Platonic love, had cherished all the time the most primitively feminine designs upon his heart and person.

This last episode is so curiously characteristic, that it seems worth while to record it in some detail. Love, according to our philosopher, played an important part in his life up to the age of forty-five. Thereafter his passions lost their urgency. Each successive spring, it is true, "aroused cravings which self-restraint, prudence and timidity prevented him from satisfying." And even in his last years he noticed in himself, and deplored, the access of low, unreasoning pride which always followed "the momentary awakening of those youthful appetites which would have humiliated me, and of which I should have feared the attacks, when I was in the prime of my strength and passions." In practice, if not invariably in desire and intention, our philosopher seems always to have been entirely blameless. Even in his forties love is wholly a matter of sentiment. "Mlle. Festa of the *Opéra Bouffe* continues to inspire in me the liveliest interest." "Today Mme. Mollien caused me to experience a tender emotion." In his fifties the remnants of his passions manifest themselves in ways even more refined. There was Mlle. Alpy, the friend, only a few years older than they, of Biran's daughters. For this charming creature our philosopher cherished a sentiment that was "more than friendship, but less than love." The days which he passed with her, in a post-chaise on the road from Paris to Périgueux, were days of unalloyed happiness. It was a kind of *Last Ride Together*, which he would have liked to prolong indefinitely.

And then there was Mme. de Caffarelli, the heroine or villainess of our cautionary story. Mme. de Caffarelli had a drawing-room in Paris and a *château* in the country, was a student of philosophy and liked to talk about religion and the occult.

Biran made her acquaintance four or five years before his death, was charmed and soon came to be infatuated. When the lady was in Paris, he invited her to meetings of the Metaphysical Society, when she was out of town he wrote her long letters and sometimes spent the weekend with her in the country. As always, however, his behaviour was entirely blameless—but blameless, as his Diary reveals, in a style that was peculiarly his own. "An elevated and truly moral man," he wrote, "should not place his happiness or unhappiness in a passion that is independent of him. He should, so far as possible, discard everything connected with the object of his sentiment and attach himself exclusively to the sentiment itself. He should cherish this sentiment in so far as he finds peace of mind through the elevated ideas, amiable emotions and generous disinterested acts inspired by the beloved object. In an advanced age, this is the only permissible kind of love." And on a later page we read that "the sentiment of pure love is the soul's whole good and its true life. When it is disobjectified, that is to say, when it has no correspondence with our sensations and imaginings, or with the objects which produce them—only then is the sentiment pure." In other words, love is pure only when the independent existence of the beloved is denied, only when a veil is drawn over the deplorable fact that she is another person, a separate centre of physical, mental and spiritual experience. Pure love, in fact, is the love inspired by the beauty of his own sentiments in the breast of Narcissus. Such are the fruits of a lifelong and exclusive habit of introspection.

As was only to be expected, Mme. de Caffarelli had no intention of being disobjectified, nor had she any desire to disobjectify her distinguished admirer. He was a great philosopher, he was full of charm, he was touching and pathetic. All the mother in her, all the *grande amoureuse*, all the Egeria went out towards him. After a time certain hints were dropped. Our philosopher began to suspect that all was not entirely as it should be. "A person whom I thought to be spiritual today denied that there could be energy without passion." He had replied, of course, that true energy is the voluntary overcoming of passion. A little later, the inevitable happened. Exactly how it happened, we are not told. All that we know is that Biran broke off his relations with the all too objective lady and asked her to return his letters. In his Diary the absurd and painful episode is thus summed up. "When a woman seems to feel the passion of love, as we men do, it almost always has a source that is impure and corrupt. It is not produced by an immediate and dominating propensity, but by levity, vanity and sensuality. Such a suspicion of Mme. de C. would have seemed to be a blasphemy. The esteem I felt for her during the first period of our friendship made me imagine that she was unlike the rest of her sex. I resisted all proofs to the contrary, and when it was impossible for me to go on believing that the person was virtuous, I fell into a living death."

The introvert, who is ignorant of the outer world, is not for that reason unaware of it. Though he *knows* very little about his fellows and the social order, he constantly *feels* them, and feels them with discomfort, as alien and often hostile presences. Hence his sense of inadequacy, of being alone, inferior, born with a different face. Like the rest of his species, Biran suffered all his life from an excruciating shyness. When, as a middle-aged man, he had his first interview with Louis XVIII, his knees trembled, his heart palpitated and his poor stomach was so painfully affected that he almost disgraced himself by being sick at the royal feet. (One of my own early memories is of a similar experience at the unveiling of my grandfather's statue by that Prince of Wales who was later to be Edward VII. My father, I recall, handed me his top-hat, just in case the worst should come to the worst. Luckily it didn't. Honour was saved; but the recollection of those moments of ghastly uncertainty are still vividly humiliating. And how much worse it must have been for the unhappy Biran! Such things are excusable in a child, as I was, of five or six. But in a widower with two marriageable daughters and a son in the army, in a member of Parliament, in an eminent philosopher, they are simply out of the question. And yet, though out of the question, such things do, in fact, occur. The horror no less than the charm of real life consists precisely in the recurrent actualization of the inconceivable.)

It did not take a king to give our philosopher stage-fright. Any and every assemblage of his fellows intimidated him. Public speaking was an agony, often a physical impossibility. Here, from the *Moniteur*, is the official report of one of our philosopher's essays in oratory. "M. Maine de Biran is called to the tribune. The weakness of the honourable member's organ not permitting him to make himself sufficiently heard, he requests M. Blanchard Bailleul to give a reading of his opinion." In the Chamber almost all Biran's eloquence was by proxy. In other places, when a speech had to be made and no friendly reader was available, he had to force himself to do his own talking. Sometimes the effort was crowned with success. Despite the "weakness of the organ," people listened and were, if not emotionally moved, at least impressed by the speaker's intelligence and honesty. But there were other times when the unhappy philosopher found himself staring at those rows of expectant faces, his head empty of ideas and his vocal cords completely paralysed. Even the most unimpressive audiences had power to inflict these humiliations upon him. As Sub-Prefect, for example, he had found himself tongue-tied when distributing prizes at a boys' school.

Biran's sense of being alien and inadequate found expression in an almost systematic avoidance of conflict and refusal to insist on his rights. Such was his dislike of argument (except on philosophical matters and then only among friends) that in a hostile group he would either keep silence or give a polite and somewhat hypocritical assent to opinions which were not his own. Where money was at stake he always preferred loss to haggling, his own disadvantage to a battle with opposing interests. To those who asked for a loan he found it almost impossible to say no, and from those to whom he had advanced money he found it no less difficult to demand repayment. His account books show that not more than one in ten of the neighbours whom he had thus obliged ever paid him back. The rest were evidently of the opinion that one should "never give a sucker an even break."

Sometimes this amiable reluctance to fight or press claims had the most disastrous results. Consider, for example, the case of Biran's daughters, Elisa and Adine. After their mother's death the two girls were placed under the care of an aunt, Mme. Gérard. Mme. Gérard was a woman of exemplary piety and diabolic character. A tyrant with the highest religious principles, a martinet in the name of virtue and Christian charity, a shrew who loved to scold and thought that she was giving utterance to righteous indignation, she was determined to have her own way in all things, to force others to bow to her will. The pleasure she took in bullying the orphans was such that, when they grew up, she refused to permit them to go and live with their father. Paris, she insisted, would be bad for their health and fatal to their morals. At Grateloup they would have to put up with a stepmother. It was essential that they should remain with their loving aunt in the prison-like house near Périgueux. Repeatedly, but always feebly, the philosopher pleaded for their liberation. But he was so much frightened of his sister-in-law, he had such a physical repugnance for the violent scenes which were her specialty, that he did not dare to insist. The rescue of the girls was postponed from month to month, from year to year. Biran loved his daughters tenderly, he longed to have them with him, he knew how passionately they hoped and prayed to be delivered. But meanwhile there was a dragon in the path and, alas, our philosopher was no St. George. Elisa and Adine were never to get out of Mme. Gérard's clutches. Their father merely wrote them long letters urging a Christian resignation to their lot. A man of less timorous disposition would have taken the unpleasant steps necessary to change that lot into one which did not call for quite so much resignation. When Biran died, the girls were still unmarried, still in custody. Adine followed her father to the grave in 1834, Elisa four years later. Their aunt, as might have been expected, was still going strong under the Second Empire.

In society Biran was always intimidated by bigwigs and successful men of affairs. Even the basest of them, even the dullest and stupidest, had power to impose on him. In their presence his self-possession evaporated; he seemed to lose his moral independence, his very reason; he found himself saying things he did not believe, doing things of which he disapproved. And all to no purpose; for they were not gratified by his abjection; they merely despised or ignored him.

With their wives and daughters our philosopher was generally somewhat more at ease. His manners were exquisite and, like his formal clothes and powdered hair, of a vintage anterior to 1789. His intimate conversation breathed a Rousseau-esque sensibility. He was seductive and yet safe, charming but perfectly reliable. But even more than the society of women our philosopher enjoyed that of his intellectual equals. Here he felt himself, and was acknowledged, the first among his peers. When it came to a philosophical discussion, this frightened underling knew how to be authoritative, this dumb and trembling orator commanded an eloquence now subtle, now incisive, now persuasively brilliant.

But finally what a relief it was, when Parliament went into its summer recess, to go home to Périgord! Here he was genuinely and unquestionably important—important, too, without effort, just because he was his grandfather's grandson, and the deputy for Bergerac, and the only metaphysician within a radius of three hundred kilometres. He did not have to make odious comparisons between himself and those younger contemporaries who were already cabinet ministers, peers of France, millionaires, Members of the Institute. He was Maine de Biran of Grateloup, whom not to know argued oneself unknown—at least at Bergerac. And then there was the second Mme. Biran—that *bonne femme* who had succeeded the *épouse celeste*. This daughter of a neighbouring squire could not write three lines without making a mistake in grammar or spelling; but she was heir to a modest estate, had a good business head, was an excellent housekeeper and could be trusted to observe the proprieties while her husband was away in Paris. Reviewing his domestic life, Biran felt that he had done very well to marry "a kind simple woman who, happy to be with me, demands nothing of me, and for whom I am always good enough as I am without making any effort to modify myself."

At home, as in the little town, nothing ever happened to make our philosopher feel inadequate or inferior. How restful, how reassuring! But when he looked into the situation a little more closely, he began to have his doubts. "If a man is distressed by his weakness, if he hates those who surpass him and seeks solitude only to avoid the humiliation of comparison, he is not humble, but full of pride."

To relieve the suffering imposed by his different face and native incapacity, the introvert resorts externally to flight, internally to an elaborately justified sense of being superior to the viscerotonic and somatotonic extraverts who are at home in the world and get on in it. "In spite of my shyness, in spite of my apparent modesty, I am tormented by pride. And pride will remain the torment of my life so long as I go on trying to satisfy only myself and my fellows and refuse to look higher to a Spirit who will direct my own spirit, or even take its place." The introvert's ambivalent attitude towards himself and the world around him is well illustrated by an earlier entry in the Diary. Here Biran records that he has spent some weeks writing and re-writing an article for Guizot's *Archives*, only to be told by the editor that his piece is too long and much too difficult for even a select public. "I am not of this world," he laments. "I ought to give up the attempt to live and work for it." But that same day he dines, as he often does, with the Abbé Morellet. Born in 1727, Morellet was the last survivor of the *philosophes*. Witty, above all at other people's expense, he had earned from Voltaire the nickname of 'l'Abbé Mord-les.' What was the bond that united this 'Reverend Bite-'em' with our gentle philosopher? Biran, as usual, drops no hint.

All we know is that on this, as on many other evenings, he accepted the old Voltairean's invitation to dinner. All went well until—how imprudently!—he started a conversation about metaphysics—"a subject which the Abbé and his circle make fun of without having the faintest idea of its nature." Such people, says Biran, "have no conception of the inner life; they regard it as mere vanity and folly. Those who know the inner life have the same opinion of the worldly, who live outside themselves. Who is the right? Those who deny what they do not know and do not wish to know? I know the outer world as well as you do, and I judge it. You know nothing of my inner world, and yet you presume to judge that world. This conversation depressed me, and I left the Abbé Morellet's feeling sad and unwell. From there I went to a soirée at the Ministry of Police."

All this is wonderfully true to type. In the morning our introvert knows too little of the outer world to be fit to live in it. In the evening he knows so much that he can pass definitive judgment on it and feel superior to the extraverts who have no knowledge of the inner life. And yet in spite of this conviction of superiority, he allows himself to be worried by old Mord-les into an indigestion —and in spite of this indigestion he hurries off to another party, at which he will feel even more of an alien than at the Abbé's. For it will be a huge and brilliant affair— men wearing decorations, women with bare shoulders and ropes of pearls. And the young ones will either look through him, as though he were not there at all; or if they look at him, will hastily conceal a smile. And no wonder! For "with a ludicrous self-complacency I adorn this ageing carcass of mine as if it could still, as in my youth, attract and tickle the world's attention." To be ludicrous, to know one is ludicrous, and yet to persist in the behaviour that causes one to be ludicrous. . . . And one calls oneself a philosopher, one cultivates the inner life, one aspires to perfection! But one mustn't be late, one mustn't be late. Tell the cabman to whip up his horse. If one goes to one's humiliation, it may as well be at the gallop.

Biran's dread of an audience extended even to the reading public. He hated to be exposed to the unsympathetic gaze of the vulgar, and hated it even when the exposure was only symbolic and on paper. Concerning his first book he wrote to a friend that "it is not without a certain terror that I find myself condemned to be printed alive." This terror remained with him, and to the end of his career publication was an ordeal to be undergone with extreme reluctance and only after long delays and a succession of second thoughts. His fear of exposure was heightened by the consciousness that he was not a born writer. He composed with difficulty, phrasing and rephrasing his ideas, but never finding a form that completely satisfied him. The right word was always something to be looked for—generally without success; it was never gratuitously given. Sentences and paragraphs did not come to him ready-made and perfect; they had to be laboriously pieced together, without inspiration and without pleasure. The product of his labours is a prose that merely permits itself to be read, never exhilarates or delights. Biran regarded his incapacity for expression as something both to be deplored and to be proud of. He lacked the gift of style and was sorry for it; but at the same time he was thankful that he was not as other authors were—a mere juggler of words. Most people, he remarks, use their minds only with the idea of letting others know the result of their labours. They never have an idea without immediately clothing it in brilliant and striking language. "The whole business of their life is the arrangement of phrases; they do all their thinking within the world of grammar and logic, and are much more concerned with forms than with substance. . . . My own sensibility," Biran goes on, "reacts but little externally. It is occupied either by confused inward impressions (this is its most habitual state), or by the ideas which strike me and which I shut up within myself to be sifted and examined, and all without feeling any need to spread them abroad. I neglect the problem of expression; I never make a phrase in my head; I study ideas for their own sake, in order to know what they are, what they imply, disinterestedly, without reference to self-love or passion. This disposition makes me eminently fit for the inner life and psychological research, but unfits me for everything else." Here, once again, we catch our introvert in the act of expressing simultaneously a sense of inadequacy and a conviction of intrinsic superiority. He laments his inability to embody his ideas in suitable language, but rejoices at the same time in the fact that he has ideas which are worth expressing, that, unlike his successful rivals, he is concerned with substance rather than form and that his concern, unlike theirs, is wholly disinterested. Comparisons are odious and painful; and yet, when they are made with sufficient care, we discover that it is the other fellow who has the worst of it.

Even if he had been physically healthy, Biran would have found himself a very difficult man to live with. But he was not healthy. An already obscure and tangled psychological situation was further darkened and complicated by the fact 'the machine,' as he liked to call it, was forever going out of order. From his parents (both of whom, incidentally, were sickly and died young) he seems to have inherited a certain weakness and instability of the nervous apparatus controlling his organic processes. It is a congenital defect for which even the highly developed medicine of the twentieth century can do very little. Biran, who was a doctor's son and the lifelong friend of doctors, subjected himself to all the rather unpleasant treatments then in vogue—emetics, purges, blisters, moxas. They did him some good; but not enough. From boyhood to the last day of his life he remained the victim of his autonomic nervous system. It tormented him, played practical jokes on him, seemed maliciously to delight in thwarting his plans and bringing his good intentions to naught. It was like an indwelling poltergeist—not I, but Flibbertigibbet in me. He would wake up in the morning, full of life and energy, mentally alert, calm and competent. A few hours later, for no apparent reason, his body was as though moribund, his mind confused, agitated, incapable of thought. And at any moment his digestion might fail him, his latent bronchitis flare up into a maddening and exhausting cough. Every change in the weather produced a corresponding change in his organism. He was one man when the barometer was high, quite another when it was low. Every existence is to some extent intermittent and discontinuous; Biran's differed from most in being extravagantly so.

Our philosopher complained a great deal of his want of health, but at the same time was aware that sickness may have its compensating advantages. "Except the sickly," he wrote in 1794, "few persons ever feel themselves existing. Those who are well, even if they be philosophers, are too busy enjoying life to investigate what it is. The sentiment of their own existence does not astonish them. Health impels us towards the outside world, sickness brings us home to ourselves." In other words, sickness conspires with the introverted temperament to create the only kind of philosopher for whom Biran had any use, the kind of philosopher he was himself—an empiricist of the personal life on all its levels from the physiological to the spiritual.

In the preceding pages I have tried to paint the portrait of our philosopher. In those which follow I shall exhibit him first in relation to history and society; next as a moralist and man of goodwill painfully wrestling with the problems of ethics; and finally, as a metaphysician who was also a candidate for enlightenment, a theorizer who felt the need to act upon his theories.

2

The Philosopher in History

Looking back into the past, we tend to imagine that people who lived at the same period of history lived effectively in the same world. But the truth is that, in any complex society, there are many worlds separated from one another by impenetrable walls of mutual ignorance and misunderstanding. Consider, for example, the case of our philosopher. Mozart was his senior by nine years;

Beethoven, four years his junior. And yet, in his *Journal*, this lover of music never so much as mentioned their names. As he grew older, Biran was increasingly preoccupied with the fact and theory of mysticism. And yet he knew nothing of Saint-Martin in France, or of the contemporary theosophists beyond the Rhine. Again, Biran was a metaphysician; but he read no German, knew Kant only through a French commentary and Kant's successors only through conversations with Victor Cousin and Stapfer. He took a keen interest in political theory; but he never cites either Fourier or Saint-Simon. With the two greatest literary figures of his day, Chateaubriand and Mme. de Staël, he did, it is true, have some personal acquaintance. But he seems to have disliked their books; at any rate he deplores the modern tendency to "a baneful melancholy and an unwholesome craving for vague emotion."

The worlds which Biran actually inhabited were, besides the world of his inner experience, the world of politics and the world of science and philosophy. The first was the showy, but depressing, world of parliamentarians and ministerial high society; the second, a world of intelligence and intelligibility, in which one discussed the nature of the self with professional metaphysicians and philosophically-minded chemists, physicists and palaeontologists; where there were doctors with whom to talk about physiology and medicine, disciples of Mesmer to tell one about animal magnetism; Pestalozzians to discourse of education.

In every historical period human beings of every kind are born and make the best of their native gifts within a cultural environment which they may find favourable or unfavourable. No single individual can ever be representative of a period, if only for physiological reasons—for a Falstaff cannot represent a constituency of Cassiuses, nor a Scrooge a group of Pickwicks. People living in one country at one time will resemble one another superficially, in so far as they exhibit the same easily recognizable peculiarities of cultural style. On the lower levels of physique and temperament, of talents, tastes and acquirements, they will be profoundly unlike one another. Resemblance begins again only on the deepest level of all, that of the spirit—of the something not ourselves which is the ground of our being.

No individual, I repeat, can be representative of his time; and our philosopher was probably rather less representative than most. Few men have lived a life so intensely personal, so constantly introverted and self-conscious. His *Journal Intime* has very little value as a historical, but very great value as a psychological document. It throws light, not on an epoch, but on a mind and temperament. Maine de Biran was not one of those who throw themselves into the life of their time with a passionate delight or a no less passionate indignation. Rather, he endured it with a kind of chronic bad grace, as one endures a trying climate, from which circumstances make it impossible to escape. And of course, if one didn't happen to like that kind of thing, life, during the Revolution and under the Empire, was no joke. It was no joke; and yet, when we read of our philosopher's encounters first with the Jacobins and later with Napoleon, we are struck, not by the ferocity, but by the forbearance displayed by the men in power. Compared with their modern counterparts, these revolutionaries of the seventeen-nineties, this military dictator of the early eighteen-hundreds, seem almost humane.

Biran was a landowner, almost a noble; he had served in the King's Bodyguard and fought against the Parisian mob. And yet this man was permitted to live out the Terror, unmolested, on his ancestral estate of Grateloup. There, in his library, he studied mathematics and philosophy; there, under the oak trees of his forest, he walked and meditated and read the works of Rousseau. And all the time his peasants continued to pay their rents and he himself went on living like the cultured gentleman that birth and breeding had made him. To his Diary he confided from time to time his thoughts about contemporary politics. They were the unrealistic thoughts of a man brought up to believe in the march of progress and amazed to discover that savagery is perfectly compatible with science, 'enlightenment' and powdered hair. Hence the vehemence of his rhetoric. Just because they were perpetrated in the age of Laplace and Lavoisier (the latter, incidentally, a victim of the Terror), the crimes of the revolutionaries seemed to Biran "a thousand times more cruel than the prescriptions of Nero and Caligula, than the massacres of the Cevennes, or Ireland, or Scotland." The blood spilt by Robespierre and his crew was sufficient "to put out all the bonfires of the Inquisition, even as it serves to efface the memory of them." But in point of fact these crimes were, quantitatively speaking, not excessive; and in point of morals, they could not be made an excuse for similar crimes committed by the opposite party. In regard to Biran himself, to his friends and compatriots, the revolutionaries had shown themselves remarkably considerate. A few of the philosopher's kinsmen and neighbours had thought it prudent to emigrate. Of those who remained in Périgord only twenty-five were condemned to death by the Revolutionary Tribunal, while only a few hundreds suffered imprisonment. The rest, like Biran, retired into private life and were left in peace.

Robespierre fell; then came the Directorate, the Consulate, the Empire. Towards the close of the Napoleonic epoch, Maine de Biran, then deputy for Bergerac, became an active member of that Commission of Five which drew up a resolution, protesting against Napoleon's tyranny and demanding a greater measure of civil and political liberty for the French people. In a Corsican fury, the Emperor denounced the Commission and dissolved the Chamber which had approved its resolution. "*La nation*," he screamed in a paroxysm of self-adoration, "*la nation a besoin de moi, et je n'ai pas besoin d'elle.*" From the satanically sublime to the ludicrous and the imbecile the step is almost infinitesimally short.

Only Napoleon's words were violent. The man who had actually written the offending resolution went quietly home to Grateloup and philosophy. When the Bourbons came back in 1814, Biran re-emerged in the nearest approach to a blaze of glory that he was ever to experience. The King and all the royal family were infinitely gracious. He was appointed Quaestor of the Chamber, with twice the salary of an ordinary deputy. Then came the return from Elba. Louis XVIII retired to Ghent, Maine de Biran to Grateloup. This time our philosopher feared the worst. But once again nothing happened. He had "a painful interview with the Prefect," followed, more satisfactorily, by a "frank explanation" with the General in command of the district—and that was all. He was free to do what he liked, provided always that he took no further part in political life.

Biran's denunciations of Napoleon are almost as indignant as those which he bestowed upon the Jacobins. His Diary, during the Hundred Days, is peppered with such words as 'usurper,' 'despot,' 'criminal.' But hell, after all, is a descending spiral; tyranny has its gradations, almost its differences in kind. Biran did not know it; but the circle, in which history had doomed him to live, was quite close to the top of the infernal pit. Under Richelieu, he would have been imprisoned or perhaps burnt for sorcery, like Urbain Grandier. And in our own days, under Mussolini, he would have been sent for seven years to an island or some dismal village in Apulia; under Hitler, he would have died in a concentration camp; under Stalin, he would have edifyingly confessed his sins before a People's Court and then have disappeared without leaving a trace even in history—for history would be falsified so as to deny him even a posthumous existence.

Bonaparte and the Jacobins lived in one of those brief Golden Ages in which even revolutionaries and dictators have their scruples and actually believe that other people—those, at least, belonging to the educated bourgeoisie—possess certain more or less inalienable rights. All this has now been changed. Under the modern dictator there is an equality of universal rightlessness. And among ever-increasing numbers of human beings this state of things is taken for granted as the normal and natural condition of man. To Napoleon, the Ideologists (among whom he mistakenly numbered our philosopher) were "a kind of vermin clinging to the skirts of my garments." But from these fierce words he did not proceed to commensurate action. Cabanis, Destutt de Tracy, Maine de Biran were only *called* vermin; there was never any question of swatting, or D.D.T., or pyrethrum. The insects were left to crawl and buzz and secrete the venom of subversive thought, with no more hindrance than was imposed by the imperial censorship and the decree which, by purging the Institute of its Class of Moral and Political Science, officially abolished a whole category of (to a dictator) most embarrassing speculation. Towards Mme. de Staël, it is true, Napoleon showed himself more severe than towards Biran and the other 'conspirators and bandits called philosophers.' In extenuation it must be admitted that that exasperating woman insistently asked for everything she got. Moreover, what she got was nothing very terrible. Exile first from Paris and finally from France was a punishment mild indeed by comparison with what would now be meted out to an ideological dissenter by an irritated tyrant.

Confronted by the facts, on the one side, of Napoleon's character and his absolute power, on the other, of Maine de Biran's complete immunity and Mme. de Staël's tempered chastisement, we find ourselves wondering why it is that, a hundred and fifty years later, we should be living in an age that has witnessed the revival of slavery, torture, forced orthodoxy and the savage persecution of heretical opinion. We can never hope to uncover all the reasons for this enormous change for the worse; but from our vantage point in time we can detect at least a few of the more obvious and important of them. It will be instructive to see how far our philosopher was aware of the tendencies which, in four or five generations, were to transform the world of Napoleon into that of Hitler and Stalin.

Let us begin with the historical movement, of whose significance and even existence Biran seems to have been most completely unaware—I mean the Industrial Revolution. In his *Journal Intime* and his various philosophical writings there is, I believe, no single reference to the sufficiently obvious fact that the structure of European economy was undergoing profound and irreversible changes. Biran was, among other things, a professional politician, and to the problems of politics he devoted many pages of his Diary and not a few considerable orations. But the notion that society might be changed more radically by a revolution in the methods of production than by a revolution in the forms of government never seems to have occurred to him. The reasons for this curious blindness are in part psychological, in part social and geographical. Our philosopher, as we have seen, had a special gift and predilection for introspection—a gift and predilection that were incompatible with any very intense or sustained interest in the external world of mere things. Moreover, this introverted metaphysician was also the proprietor of an estate in one of the most exclusively agricultural areas of France. In so far as he took an interest in mere things, he took it in things connected with the woods and vineyards, the cattle and pastures of his native Périgord. His material and spiritual homes were Grateloup and psychology, Paris and the politics of moderate royalism. Of Lille and Lyons and their proliferating industrial slums, of the new steam-engines and the new factories with their expensive machinery and their regimented workers, he knew and cared nothing at all.

The fact seems less surprising when we remember the curious case of Biran's contemporary, François-Charles

Fourier. Fourier was a man of excellent intelligence, who had seen the new industrial methods in action and had spent the whole of his adult life thinking about the organization of society and the production and distribution of wealth. And yet, writing in the second and third decades of the nineteenth century, he could express the belief that the problems of rapid transport would be solved by the breeding of new species of preternaturally nimble draught animals. And this at a time when Stephenson's 'Rocket' had already outstripped the horse.

When Maine de Biran looked into the future, he saw unpleasant visions of insubordination, revolution, anarchy and finally military dictatorship. And he saw clearly; for every outburst of collective violence always results in a more or less prolonged diminution of individual liberty. What he did not perceive was the more insidious threat to the freedom and dignity of man inherent in the new techniques of production. A human being is a not very strong animal possessed of a mind that in its higher reaches is spontaneously creative and capable of apprehending modes of existence that are 'not of this world.' Such a creature cannot, by its very nature, be continuously efficient. A machine, on the contrary, is designed to be efficient all the time. When a man is put in charge of a machine, or when he becomes part of some social or economic organization that is modelled upon the machine, he is compelled to be what it is not natural or normal for him to be. In more than moderate doses efficiency is incompatible with humanity.

But in a world of advanced technology efficiency tends to become the end, to which men and women are the means. The machine sets an unattainable sub-human standard; organizations and individuals are expected to conform to that standard. Failure to reach it is punished. Under democratic dispensations the punishment is relatively mild and consists in being relegated to the class of the unskilled or even of the unemployable. Under the modern totalitarian dictatorship—a régime dedicated to the pursuit of military efficiency—inefficiency receives a shorter shrift.

In this context let me quote the words of a modern French philosopher, whose thought has many affinities with that of Maine de Biran—I mean, M. Gabriel Marcel. "Such practices as the liquidation of incurables or, during the war, the extermination of slaves who had reached a degree of exhaustion, beyond which they could no longer earn their pittance miserable as it was, practices justly regarded as monstrous and inhuman, are now seen to be the irrefutably logical results of a given point of view" —the point of view of the efficiency expert. "Such practices still, thank God, excite general indignation. But it is to be feared that this is so only because mankind is not yet sufficiently adapted to a world of pure technics; and we are forced to recognize that on this road, which leads to the most appalling barbarism—a barbarism supported by reasoning—a good many stages have already been passed." Biran's contemporaries were galloping enthusiastically along the early stages of that road. Twenty-five years after our philosopher's death Karl Marx began his denunciations of capitalist inhumanity. During the next seventy-five years trade unionism and liberal legislation did much to mitigate that inhumanity. Then came war, revolution, economic dislocation. The threat of anarchy was made an excuse for the concentration of power in the hands of a ruling oligarchy. And meanwhile a developing technology had created ideals of efficiency more sub-humanly remote from life than at any previous time. Men and women were expected to live up, or rather down, to standards set by machines and machine-like organizations of a hitherto unheard-of perfection. And if they failed to do so, there at their heels was the State; and the State was equipped with every modern convenience from machine-guns to tape-recorders and concealed microphones.

To Biran, the most disturbing thing about the man who had run the secret police under Napoleon and who, in 1815, was doing the same dirty work for Louis XVIII, was his total lack of principle, his readiness to do anything for money and power. It seems never to have occurred to him that Fouché might be more alarming on account of his intellectual qualities than of his moral defects—more dangerous because he was so businesslike and efficient than because he was a low intriguing blackmailer. Still less did it occur to our philosopher that, with the general advance in science and technology, the ability of any government to spy and eavesdrop, to regiment and coerce, to suppress or fabricate opinions, to withhold truth and inculcate falsehood, was likely to increase—to go on increasing until it would become very difficult for men to think unorthodox thoughts and quite impossible for them to carry through a successful rebellion.

The Industrial Revolution was not the only great historical movement of whose significance our philosopher remained more or less completely unaware. There was also nationalism. Maine de Biran was a good Frenchman;

but he was also a good legitimist and a good European of the pre-Revolution variety. Hence his inability to understand the modern frenzies of chauvinism at home and, abroad, of Young Germanism, nascent Italianism, Holy Russia-ism, British Empire-ism. During the Hundred Days we find him calmly deploring the fact that the great majority of his compatriots were praying for the success, not of the Cossacks and the English, but of the tyrant and his detestable soldiery. "We forget that the most dangerous enemy is the one who will remain to devour us, whereas the others will go their way. We are a flock of sheep, allying ourselves with the tiger against the lions who are at war with him; we do not reflect that, when he has made use of us to expel his personal enemies, he will turn and rend us with his blood-stained claws." To Maine de Biran the nationalist's first principle—that 'we' are right and 'they' are always wrong—was by no means self-evident. He admired the magnanimity of the Allies, and considered that the national honour was safe in the keeping of these generous conquerors, who had delivered France from her servitude to 'the modern Attila.' That nationalistic idolatry was destined to become the effective religion of the twentieth century was a fact which his temperament and upbringing made it impossible for Biran to foresee. Once again he was not the only bad prophet. A generation after his death even so shrewd an observer as Karl Marx could gravely underestimate the importance of nationalism. Marx thought that local patriotism was destined very soon to be replaced by class patriotism. The idea that communism might one day become, not the ideological, emotional and political substitute for nationalism, but an instrument in the service of a particular nation and empire, never seems to have occurred to him. Marx's contemporary, Mazzini, had a clearer sense of the power, the enduring historical significance of nationalism. But Mazzini was so completely blinded by his humanitarian idealism and his personal experience of foreign oppression, that he could not recognize the intrinsically evil and destructive nature of nationalism. Within five years of achieving its liberty every oppressed nationality takes to militarism, and within two or three generations, sometimes within a single generation, it becomes, if circumstances are propitious, an imperialist aggressor, eager to inflict upon its neighbours the oppression of which itself was so recently a victim.

Biran often complained that he had been born too late, and he looked back with nostalgic envy to the great age of French literature and philosophy, when the native genius of a Fossuet, a Fénelon, a Malebranche had been reinforced, had been given purpose and direction by a system of unshakable beliefs. By ruining this system of beliefs, the 'nothing-but' philosophies of the eighteenth century had weakened men's creative energies, leaving them empty and unfruitful. Biran did not see that nature's abhorrence for a vacuum is as strong in the mental as in the material world. Men cannot live in a chronic state of negation; the voids of thought and feeling must be filled, and if we reject the divine, its place will inevitably be taken by some idolatrous *ersatz*. Even when the belief in God is universally accepted, the worship of a God-substitute may, in fact, be the effective religion of some men all the time and of all men some of the time. Consider, for example, organized Christianity. This has always been a mixed religion, in which one part of God-worship was combined with four or five parts of idolatrous Church-worship and two or three parts of fetishism. With the decline of Christianity, such God-worship as had existed went out; the idolatrous worship of the Church was exchanged for the equally idolatrous worship of the State and the Nation; and, diverted from relics, images and hallowed formulas, the cult of fetishes came to be directed upon such things as flags, national anthems and the slogans of political and economic theory. The revolutionary period and the Empire provide early examples of this secular and wholly unmitigated idolatry; but the full development of the new religion has been reserved for our own century. The 'nothing-but' philosophies associated with the advance of technology have now come to seem almost axiomatically true. In the high vacuum of the modern world not a trace of the divine or the eternal remains, and the notions of State, Nation and Party are therefore free to expand into vast and monstrous caricatures of God. In the service of this God-surrogate and of his prophet, Efficiency, totalitarian dictators find it right and proper to behave with systematic savagery. In the democratic countries we worship the same deity and prophet, but under the influence of an old irrelevant habit we neglect to draw the practical conclusions which logically flow from the premises of nationalism and technics. M. Marcel is evidently of the opinion that the inner logic of our idolatry will soon prove irresistible; and Mr. George Orwell even assigns a date to our impending conversion. In 1984 we shall all be living under totalitarian conditions.

Closely associated with nation-worship and the cult of

efficiency, and hardly less fruitful of evil than they, is faith in inevitable progress and the redemptive power of history to save humanity in some more or less distant future. Biran seems to have started out with a standard eighteenth-century belief in all-round progress. The Terror startled him into reconsidering that belief, and by the time Bonaparte had risen to fame as the conqueror of Italy, he was most uncertain whether scientific and technological progress is inevitably correlated with improvement in behaviour. The news of the wanton extinction of the Venetian Republic set him thinking of the *jus gentium*, as formulated by Grotius and Montesquieu. Great men! And what they wrote had been true and fine. "But in practice what has been the use of it all? Has it made us more just in conquest, more humane and reasonable in victory? What is now happening in Italy proves the contrary." One is reminded of the words which Herodotus put into the mouth of the Persian who talked with Thersander at Thebes. "Of all man's miseries the bitterest is this, to know so much and to have control over nothing." Doubting the inevitability and all-roundness of progress, Biran came to feel very dubious about that Future to which the Liberals looked forward with such sanguine hope and for which the revolutionaries were prepared to sacrifice so much present good, so many contemporary lives and liberties.

But how could these people feel so cocksure about the future? Except to a very limited extent, the future is unpredictable, and nobody can form more than the vaguest idea of the more distant consequences of his present actions. The best laid plans have results which no planner, however intelligent, can foresee. These are matters of everyday experience. And yet the revolutionaries and the advocates of radical reforms implicitly deny the fact of man's necessary ignorance. They claim infallibility not, like the Pope, about dogma, but in regard to the events of tomorrow and next year. In the light of this pretended knowledge they assert that their plans will result in happiness for generations yet unborn. And this future happiness will be so enormous as to justify retrospectively the infliction of present misery without compunction and on the largest scale.

Biran concludes his reflections on the Liberals of 1820 with the remark that "Robespierre and Napoleon reasoned in this way." And, more than a century later, so did Hitler and Mussolini and the Japanese war lords; so do Stalin and the lesser dictators of today. Modern tyrants differ from their counterparts in antiquity inasmuch as they are all convinced believers in Progress, in a hypostatized and almost personified History that is providentially 'on our side,' and in a Future so gorgeous that no present price for its attainment can be regarded as excessive. Five or six millions must be liquidated, a hundred millions reduced to slavery. What of it? In the twenty-second century their great-great-grandchildren will be men like gods.

Men like gods. But can it be that the printer has made a mistake? Shouldn't that final word be 'dogs'? For obviously, if the attempt be made to fashion humanity's better future by means that are consistently anti-human, the end-product is likely to be something much nearer to the well-kicked animal than to Apollo or Hermes. This was a fact which our philosopher understood very well. He had seen that large-scale violence leads either directly, or through anarchy, to tyranny, and this knowledge made him a moderate in politics, a lover of peace and quiet with a decided preference for a constitutional King Log over any kind of King Stork, whether of the extreme right or the extreme left. Sentimentally attached to the legitimate dynasty, he was yet no friend of the future Charles X or of his reactionary supporters. Their antics, he saw, might easily crack the thin precarious crust of decency, which is all that separates any civilization, however impressive, from the hells of anarchy or systematic tyranny which lie in wait beneath the surface. Biran had read the story of Alypius in St. Augustine's *Confessions*, he had watched, from a safe hiding-place, the career of Robespierre, had served and suffered under Bonaparte; through books and at first-hand he knew that, though it may be temperament and childhood frustration that make the sadist and the despot, it is adult opportunity that finally actualizes these monsters and imposes them upon society. Suppress the opportunities and you will stop up a principal source of injustice and eliminate the sufferings associated with tyranny and paranoia in high places. And since the opportunities for tyranny and systematic sadism are most plentiful during times of social unrest, civil strife and international war, it follows that the only reasonable policy is one of peace and order at almost any price. To this basic principle Biran was unwaveringly attached; but that attachment, ironically enough, imparted to his political career a course so consistently wobbly that the peasants of his constituency, changing the B of his name into a V, used to speak of him as *Monsieur Viran*.

Despite all appearances, they were unjust; for our

philosopher was no weathercock, but rather a compass needle steadily pointing towards moderation. But unfortunately this pointing had to be done in relation to existing parties and policies. Thus, in 1814, we find him siding with the Ultras, whom he regarded as the staunchest supporters of legitimacy and order. By the end of 1815 he had realized that these extreme royalists were dangerous revolutionaries, who threatened the hardly won tranquillity of France and were as greedy for power and as impatient of constitutional restraint as Bonaparte or the Jacobins. In consequence of this discovery he began to work with the Liberals. But the Liberals wanted to change too much too quickly, and were altogether too democratic for the taste of an aristocratic intellectual. Biran was no believer in the virtue or wisdom of "the People," whom he regarded as a mere "collection of ignorant and passionate individuals, who act only under the impulse of blind emotion." The idea of the sovereign People was absurd. Sovereignty should be vested in a royal house, wielding an authority guaranteed by sentiment and tradition, but hedged about by a constitution and acting under advice from the representatives of the educated minority. The Liberals aimed at undermining the authority of the King and handing over more power to the People—or, to be more accurate, of using the People to increase the power of the bourgeois-industrial class to which they themselves belonged. Regarding them as the more dangerous threat to stability, Biran swung back towards the side of the Ultras. But, needless to say, the Ultras had learnt nothing and forgotten nothing, and by 1820 he was even more heartily disgusted by them than he had been in 1815.

He then came to disapprove and be disapproved by practically everybody in French politics. It was an uncomfortable but not at all discreditable position—a position analogous to that which another philosopher, Erasmus, had occupied, two centuries before, between the Reformers and the ecclesiastical conservatives. "A plague on both your houses" is the motto of all moderates.

That Biran should have been only dimly and partially aware of the historical forces at work in his society is not at all surprising. Even philosophers, even professional politicians do most of their living on the individual plane, knowing little (and generally caring even less) about the vast, vague movements taking place on the subpersonal levels of history and society, of long durations and large numbers. Biran had his blind spots and his illusions. But so did even the acutest of his contemporaries. The Ideologists, for example, lived in a fairyland of optimistic rationalism. The Ultras dreamed of a future that should be like the mediaeval past—or, to be more accurate, like their fantastic ideas of the mediaeval past. James Mill, who thought of himself as a stern, hard realist, was convinced that teaching everybody to read would, simply by exposing the electors to the arguments in favour of democracy, guarantee political liberty forever. Biran may have been strangely blind and in some respects strangely ingenuous; but at least he could see through these absurdities. He knew that the Ideologists were hopelessly sunk in that Original Sin of the intellect, over-simplification. He knew that the Romantics and the Ultras were deliberately shutting their eyes to contemporary facts. And he knew the psychological baselessness of Mill's faith in primary education. Not, of course, that he had the faintest premonition of Harmsworth or Hearst, of modern advertising or the comic strip, of Goebbels or Tass. It was rather that Biran had studied his own mind too closely to be able to believe that human beings are guided in their actions by enlightened self-interest.

Systematic knowledge of historical trends and 'waves of the future' is sought only by the intellectual few. But every individual lives here and now, and is more or less profoundly affected by the fact that now is not then, nor here somewhere else. What are, and what should be, the relations between the personal and the historical, the existential and the social? Biran never posed this question in so many words; consequently we have to infer his answers from what he says in other contexts. What he seems to suggest, throughout the *Journal Intime*, is that the individual's relation to history and society is normally that of victim to monster. This being so, every reasonable person should try, so far as he can, to escape from history—but into what? Into abstract thought and the inner life, or else (and this was the conclusion reached by our philosopher towards the end of his career) into the loving contemplation of the divine Spirit.

The problem is so important that it deserves a more thorough examination than Biran chose to give it. Let us begin with an analogy drawn from inanimate matter. The laws of gases are concerned with the interdependence of volume, pressure and temperature. But the individual molecules of which the gas is composed have neither temperature nor pressure, but only kinetic energy and a tendency to random movement. In a word, the laws of single molecules are entirely different from the laws of the gases they constitute. Something of the same kind is true of individuals and societies. In groups consisting of large numbers of human individuals, certain regularities can be detected and certain sociological laws can be formulated. Because of the relatively small size of even the most considerable human groups, and because of the enormous differences, congenital and acquired, between individual and individual, these regularities have numerous exceptions and these sociological laws are rather inexact. But this is no reason for dismissing them. For, in the words of Edgar Zilser, from whose essay on *The Problems of Empiricism* I have borrowed this simile of molecules and gases, "no physicist or astronomer would disregard a regularity on the ground that it did not always hold."

For our purposes the important thing about sociological laws is not their inexactness but the fact that they are quite different from the psychological and physiological laws which govern the individual person. "If," says Zilser, "we look for social regularities by means of empathy"—feeling ourselves into a situation by imagining what would be our own behaviour in regard to it—"we may never find them, since ideas, wishes and actions might not appear in them at all." In a word, changes in quantity, if sufficiently great, result in changes in kind. Between the individual and the social, the personal and the historical, there is a difference amounting to incommensurability. Nobody now reads Herbert Spencer's *Man versus the State.* And yet the conflict between what is good for a psycho-physical person and what is good for an organization wholly innocent of feelings, wishes and ideas, is real and seems destined to remain forever unresolved. One of the many reasons for the bewildering and tragic character of human existence is the fact that social organization is at once necessary and fatal. Men are forever creating such organizations for their own convenience and forever finding themselves the victims of their home-made monsters. History reveals the Church and the State as a pair of indispensable Molochs. They protect their worshipping subjects, only to enslave and destroy them. The relations between social organizations and the individuals who live under them is symbolically expressed by the word 'shepherd,' as applied to the priests and rulers, who like to think of themselves as God's earthly representatives, and even to God Himself. The metaphor is of high, but not the highest, antiquity; for it was first used by the herd-owning, land-destroying, meat-eating and war-waging peoples who replaced the horticulturists of the first civilization and put an end to that Golden Age of Peace, which not long since was regarded as a mere myth, but is now revealed by the light of archaeology as a proto- and pre-historical reality. By force of unreflecting habit we go on talking sentimentally about the Shepherd of His people, about Pastors and their flocks, about stray lambs and a Good Shepherd. We never pause to reflect that a shepherd is 'not in business for his health,' still less for the health of his sheep. If he takes good care of the animals, it is in order that he may rob them of their wool and milk, castrate their male offspring and finally cut their throats and convert them into mutton. Applied to most of the States and Churches of the last two or three thousand years, this pastoral metaphor is seen to be exceedingly apt—so apt, indeed, that one wonders why the civil and ecclesiastical herders of men should ever have

Maine de Biran

allowed it to gain currency. From the point of view of the individual lambs, rams and ewes there is, of course, no such thing as a *good* shepherd; their problem is to find means whereby they may enjoy the benefits of a well-ordered social life without being exposed to the shearings, milkings, geldings and butcheries which have always been associated with the pastoral office. To discuss those means would lead us too far afield. Let it suffice to say that, given, first, the manifest unfitness of almost all human beings to exercise much power for very long, and, second, the tendency for social institutions to become pseudo-divine ends, to which individual men and women are merely means, it follows that every grant of authority should be hedged about with effective reservations; that political, economic and religious organizations should be small and co-operative, never large, and therefore inhuman and hierarchical; that the centralization of economic and political power should be avoided at all costs; and that nations and groups of nations should be organized as federations of local and professional bodies, having wide powers of self-government. At the present time, unfortunately, all signs point, not to decentralization and the abolition of man-herders, but rather to a steady increase in the power of the Big Shepherd and his oligarchy of bureaucratic dogs, to a growth in the size, the complexity, the machine-like efficiency and rigidity of social organizations, and to a completer deification of the State, accompanied by a completer reification, or reduction to thing-hood, of individual persons.

Maine de Biran's temperament was such that, even when he found himself on the winning side, even when he was an official personage of some importance, he continued to regard the social and the historical with the same apprehensive dislike as he had felt towards them in the days of Bonaparte and the Jacobins. In his Diary the longing to escape from his pigeon-hole in the social hierarchy, to break out of contemporary history and return to a purely private life, is expressed almost as frequently as the longing to be delivered from the body of this death. And yet he remained to the end embedded in politics and chained to his legislative functions. Why? To begin with, our philosopher was far from rich and found it very hard, without his official salary, to make both ends meet. Next there was his sense of duty. He felt morally obliged to do all he could for the royal house and for his rustic neighbours in Périgord. And finally there was his very unphilosophical desire to seem important, to be a personage among the pompous personages of the great world. Groaning and reluctant, yet perennially hopeful of the miracle that should transform him from a tongue-tied introvert into the brilliant and commanding herder of men, he went on clinging to his barbed perch among the great. It was death, and not his own will, that finally relaxed that agonizing clutch.

Fortunately for Biran, his martyrdom was not continuous. Even at moments when history pressed upon him most alarmingly, he found it possible to take a complete holiday in abstract thought. Sometimes he did not even have to *take* his holiday; it came to him, spontaneously, gratuitously, in the form of an illumination, or a kind of ecstasy. Thus, to our philosopher the spring of 1794 was memorable not for the executions of Hébert and Danton, not because Robespierre had now dedicated the Terror to the greater glory of the Supreme Being, but on account of an event that had nothing whatever to do with history or the social environment. "Today, the twenty-seventh of May, I had an experience too beautiful, too remarkable by its rarity ever to be forgotten. I was walking by myself a few minutes before sundown. The weather was perfect; spring was at its freshest and most brilliant; the whole world was clothed in that charm which can be felt by the soul, but not described in words. All that struck my senses filled my heart with a mysterious, sad sweetness. The tears stood in my eyes. Ravishment succeeded ravishment. If I could perpetuate this state, what would be lacking to my felicity? I should have found upon this earth the joys of heaven."

During the Hundred Days Biran was a good deal closer to history than he had been at Grateloup in 1794. Every event that occurred between the return from Elba and Waterloo filled him with a bitter indignation. "I am no longer kind, for men exasperate me. I can now see only criminals and cowards. Pity for misfortune, the need to be useful and to serve my fellows, the desire to relieve distress, all the expansive and generous sentiments which were, up till now, my principles of action, are suffering a daily diminution in my heart."

Such are the ordinary psychological consequences of violent events on the historical level. Individuals react to these events with a chronic uncharitableness punctuated by paroxysms of hate, rage and fear. Happily, in the long run, malice is always self-destructive. If it were not, this earth would be, not a Middle World of inextricably mingled good and evil, but plain, unmitigated Hell. In the short run, however, the war-born uncharitableness of many individuals constitutes a public opinion in favour of yet more collective violence.

In Biran's case the bitterness with which he reacted to contemporary history filled only his heart. "My mind, meanwhile, is occupied with abstract speculations, foreign to all the interests of this world. The speculations keep me from thinking about my fellow men—and this is fortunate; for I cannot think of them except to hate and despise."

The life of every individual occupies a certain position in time, is contemporary with certain political events and runs parallel, so to speak, with certain social and cultural movements. In a word, the individual lives surrounded by history. But to what extent does he actually live *in* history? And what precisely is this history by which individuals are surrounded and within which each of them does at least some of his living?

Let us begin by considering the second of these two questions: What *is* history? Is history something which exists, in its intelligible perfection, only in the minds of historians? Or is it something actually experienced by the men and women who are born into time, live out their lives, die and are succeeded by their sons and daughters?

Mr. Toynbee puts the question somewhat differently: "What," he asks, "will be singled out as the salient event of our time by future historians? Not, I fancy, any of those sensational or tragic or catastrophic political and economic events which occupy the headlines of our newspapers and the foregrounds of our minds," but rather "the impact of Western civilization upon all the other societies of the world," followed by the reaction (already perceptible) of those other civilizations upon Western civilization and the ultimate emergence of a religion affirming "the unity of mankind." This is an answer to our question as well as to Mr. Toynbee's. For, obviously, the processes he describes are not a part of anybody's immediate experience. Nobody now living is intimately aware of them; nobody feels that they are happening to himself or sees them happening to his children or his friends. But the (to a philosophical historian) unimportant tragedies and catastrophes, which fill the headlines, actually happen to some people, and their repercussions are part of the experience of almost everybody. If the philosophical historians are right, everything of real importance in history is a matter of very long durations and very large numbers. Between these and any given person, living at any given moment of time, lie the events predominantly 'tragic or catastrophic,' which are the subject matter of unphilosophical history. Some of these events can become part of the immediate experience of persons; and, conversely, some persons can to some extent modify the tragedies and control the catastrophes. Inasmuch as they involve fairly large numbers and fairly long durations, such events are a part of history. But from the philosophical historian's point of view they are important only in so far as they are at once the symptoms of a process involving much greater numbers and longer durations, and the means to the realization of that process. Individuals can never actually experience the long-range process, which, according to the philosophical historians, gives meaning to history. All that they can experience (and this experience is largely sub-conscious) is the circumambient culture. And should they be intellectually curious, they can discover, through appropriate reading, that the culture by which they are surrounded is different in certain respects from the culture which surrounded their ancestors. Between one state of a culture and another later state there is not, and there cannot be, a continuity of experience. Every individual simply finds himself where in fact he is—here, not there; now, not then. Necessarily ignorant of the meaningful processes of long-range history, he has to make the best of that particular tract of short-range tragedy and catastrophe, that particular section of a cultural curve, against which his own personal life traces its organic pattern of youth, maturity and decay. Once again, it is a case of the gas and its constituent molecules. Gas laws are not the same as the laws governing the particles within the gas. Though he himself must act, suffer and enjoy as a molecule, the philosophical historian does his best to think as a gas—or rather (since a society is incapable of thought) as the detached observer of a gas. It is, of course, easy enough to take the gaseous view of a period other than one's own. It is much more difficult to take it in regard to the time during which one is oneself a molecule within the social gas. That is why a modern historian feels himself justified in revising the estimates of their own time made by the authors of his documents—in correcting, for example, the too unfavourable view of the age of Aquinas and the cathedral-builders taken by all thirteenth-century moralists, or the too favourable view of industrial civilization taken by many Victorian moralists.

History as something experienced can never be fully recorded. For, obviously, there are as many such histories as there have been experiencing human beings. The nearest approach to a general history-as-something-experienced would be an anthology of a great variety of personal documents. Professor Coulton has compiled a number of excellent anthologies of this kind covering the mediaeval period. They should be read by anyone who wants to know, not what modern historians think about the Middle Ages, but what it actually felt like to be a contemporary of St. Francis, or Dante, or Chaucer.

History-as-something-experienced being unwritable, we must perforce be content with history-as-something-in-the-minds-of-historians. This last is of two kinds: the short-range history of tragedies and catastrophes, political ups and downs, social and economic revolutions; and the long-range, philosophical history of those very long durations and very large numbers, in which it is possible to observe meaningful regularities, recurrent and developing patterns. No two philosophical historians discover precisely the same regularities or meanings; and even among the writers of the other kind of history there is disagreement in regard to the importance of the part played by individuals in the short-range political and economic movements, which are their chosen subject matter. These divergencies of opinion are unfortunate, but, in view of our present ignorance, inevitable.

We may now return to the first of our two questions. To what extent does the individual, who lives surrounded by history, actually live in history? How much is his existence conditioned by the sociologists' trinity of Place, Work and Folk? How is he related to the circumambient culture? In what ways is his molecular personality affected by the general state of the social gas, and his own position within it? The answer, it is evident, will be different in each particular case; but it is possible, none the less, to cast up a reckoning sufficiently true to average experience to have at least some significance for every one of us.

Let us begin with the obvious but none the less very strange fact that all human beings pass nearly a third of their lives in a state that is completely non-historical, non-social, non-cultural—and even non-spatial and non-temporal. In other words, for eight hours out of every twenty-four they are asleep. Sleep is the indispensable condition of physical health and mental sanity. It is in sleep that our body repairs the damage caused by the day's work and the day's amusements; in sleep that the *vis medicatrix naturae* overcomes our disease; in sleep that our conscious mind finds some respite from the cravings and aversions, the fears, anxieties and hatreds, the planning and calculating which drive it during waking hours to the brink of nervous exhaustion and sometimes beyond. Many of us are chronically sick and more or less far gone in neurosis. That we are not much sicker and much madder than we are is due exclusively to that most blessed and blessing of all natural graces, sleep. Even a Himmler, even a Marquis de Sade, even a Jay Gould and a Zaharoff must resign themselves to being, during thirty per cent. of their existence, innocent, sane and obscurely at one with the divine ground of all being. One of the most dreadfully significant facts about political, social and ecclesiastical institutions is that they never sleep. In so far as individual human beings create and direct them, they embody the ideals and the calculating cleverness, inextricably combined with the conscious or unconscious cravings, aversions and fears, of a group of waking selves. Every large organization exists in a state of chronic insomnia and so can never receive directly those accessions of new life and wisdom which, in dreams and dreamless unconsciousness, come sometimes trickling, sometimes pouring in from the depths of the sleeper's being or even from some source beyond those depths. An institution can be revivified only by individuals who, because they are capable of sleep and inspiration, are capable of becoming more than themselves.

The enlightened person, as the word 'Buddha' implies, is fully and forever awake—but with a wakefulness radically different from that of the social organization; for he is awake even during the day to that which the unregenerate can approach only in sleep, that which social organizations never approach at all. When such organizations are left to their insomnia, when they are permitted to function according to the laws of their own being, subordinating individual insights to collective tradition, they become mad—not like an individual lunatic, but with a solemn, traditional and systematic madness that is at once majestic and ludicrous, grotesque and terrifying. There is a hymn which exhorts us to thank God that the Church unsleeping her watch is keeping. Instead of rejoicing in the fact we should lament and deplore. Unsleeping, the Church kept watch, century after century, over its bank accounts, its lands, its prestige, its political influence, its idolatrously worshipped dogmas, rites and traditions. All the enormous evils and imbecilities recorded in ecclesiastical history are the products of this fatal incapacity of a social organization to go to sleep.

Conversely all the illuminations and charities of personal religion have their source in the Spirit, which transcends and yet is the most inward ground of our own being, and with which, gratuitously in sleep, and in moments of insight and illumination prepared for by a deliberate 'dying to self,' the individual spirit is able to establish contact.

One culture gives us the pyramids, another the Escorial, a third, Forest Lawn. But the act of dying remains always and everywhere identical. Like sleep, death is outside the pale of history—a molecular experience unaffected by the state of the social gas. Every individual has to die alone, to die by himself to himself. The experience cannot be shared; it can only be privately undergone. "How painful it is," writes Shestov, "to read Plato's account of the last days of Socrates! His hours are numbered, and he talks, talks, talks. . . . That is what comes of having disciples. They won't allow you even to die in peace. The best death is the death we consider the worst, when one is alone, far from home, when one dies in the hospital like a dog in a ditch. Then at least one cannot spend one's last moments pretending, talking, teaching. One is allowed to keep silence and prepare oneself for the terrible and perhaps specially important event. Pascal's sister reports that he, too, talked a great deal before he died. Musset, on the contrary, wept like a child. May it not be that Socrates and Pascal talked as much as they did because they were afraid of crying?"

Hardly less unhistorical than death is old age. Modern medicine has done something to make the last years of a long life a little more comfortable, and pension plans have relieved the aged of a dependence upon charity or their children. Nevertheless, in spite of vitamins and social security, old age is still essentially what it was for our ancestors—a period of experienced decline and regression, to which the facts of contemporary history, the social and economic movements of the day, are more or less completely irrelevant. The ageing man of the middle twentieth century lives, not in the public world of atomic physics and conflicting ideologies, of welfare states and supersonic speed, but in his strictly private universe of physical weakness and mental decay.

It was the same with our philosopher. Laplace was his older contemporary, Cuvier and Ampère were his friends. But his last years were lived, not in the age of scientific progress which history records, but in the intimate experience of dying ever more completely to love, to pleasure, to enthusiasm, to sensibility, even to his intellect. "The most painful manner of dying to oneself," he writes, "is to be left with only so much of a reflective personality as suffices to recognize the successive degradation of those faculties, on account of which one could feel some self-esteem." Compared with these facts of his immediate experience, the social and the historical seemed unimportant.

Progress is something that exists on the level of the species (as increasing freedom from and control over natural environment) and perhaps also on the level of the society or the civilization (as an increase in prosperity, knowledge and skill, an improvement in laws and manners). For the individual it does not exist, except as an item of abstract knowledge. Like the other trends and movements recorded in books of history-as-something-in-the-mind-of-the historian, it is never an object of individual experience. And this for two reasons. The first of these must be sought in the fact that man's organic life is intrinsically non-progressive. It does not keep on going up and up, in the manner of the graphs representing literacy, or national income, or industrial production. On the contrary, it is a curve like a flattened cocked hat. We are born, rise through youth to maturity, continue for a time on one level, then drop down through old age and decrepitude into death. An ageing member of even the most progressive society experiences only molecular decay, never gaseous expansion.

The second reason for the individual's incapacity to experience progress is purely psychological and has nothing to do with the facts of physiology. Most human beings have an almost infinite capacity for taking things for granted. By the mere fact of having come into existence, the most amazing novelty becomes in a few months, even a few days, a familiar and, as it were, self-evident part of the environment. Every aspiration is for a golden ceiling overhead; but the moment that ceiling has been reached, it becomes a commonplace and disregarded floor, on which we dance or trudge in a manner indistinguishable, so far as our feeling-tone is concerned, from that in which we danced and trudged on the floor below. Moreover, every individual is born into a world having a social and technological floor of a particular kind, and is completely unaware, except through reading and by hearsay, that there was ever any other kind of floor. Between the members of one generation and the members of the preceding and subsequent generations there is no continuity of immediate experience. This means that one can read or write books about progress, but that one cannot feel it or live it in the same way as one feels a pain or lives one's old age.

Sleep and old age account for about thirty years of our

allotted three score and ten. In other words, nearly half of every life is passed either completely outside of the social and the historical, or in a world of enforced privacy, to which the social and the historical are only slightly relevant. Like the experience of old age, the experience of sickness takes the individual out of history and society. This does not mean, of course, that history is without effect on the bodily and mental health of individuals. What it does mean, however, is that, though certain diseases are less common and less dangerous than in the past, though hospitals are better and medical treatment more rational, sickness still causes an alienation from the world of history, and that, while it lasts, this alienation is as complete as ever it was in the past. Moreover, in spite of the progress in hygiene and medicine, in spite of the elimination from many parts of the earth of the contagious diseases which used to plague our forefathers, sickness is still appallingly common. Chronic, degenerative ailments are on the increase, and so are mental disorders, ranging from mild neuroses, with their accompanying physical disabilities, to severe and often incurable psychoses. Our fever hospitals are empty, but our asylums are full to bursting. Thanks to events which can be recorded in social history, a person living in the twentieth century is much less likely to catch the plague than was a person living in the fourteenth, but rather more likely to develop cancer, diabetes, coronary disease, hypertension, neurosis, psychosis and all the varieties of psycho-somatic disorders.

Like death, sickness has had a great variety of cultural concomitants; but these changing concomitants have not changed the essential fact that sick persons experience an alienation from their culture and society, that they temporarily fall out of history into their private world of pain and fever.

Thus, because Biran was a child of the century which had perfected the chronometer and the clock-work flute player, he always, though a strenuous anti-mechanist, referred to his body as 'the machine.' And because St. Francis had been brought up in thirteenth-century Umbria, among peasants and their beasts, he always referred to *his* body as 'Brother Ass.' Differences in place, work and folk account for these differences in terminology. But when 'the machine' suffered, it suffered in just the same way as 'Brother Ass' had suffered nearly six hundred years before, in just the same way as St. Paul's 'body of this death' had suffered in the first century.

Sickness, then, and old age take us out of history. Does this mean that the young and the healthy are permanently in history? Not at all. In the normal person, all the physiological processes are in their nature unhistorical and incommunicably non-social. The arts of breathing and assimilation, for example, of regulating body temperature and the chemistry of the blood, were acquired before our ancestors were even human. Digestion and excretion have no history; they are always there, as given facts of experience, as permanent elements in the destiny of every individual man and woman who has ever lived. The pleasures of good and the discomforts of bad digestion are the same at all times, in all places, under whatever political régime or cultural dispensation.

Maine de Biran, as we learn from his *Journal*, had a very delicate and capricious digestion. When it worked well, he found life worth living and experienced a sense of well-being which made even a dinner party at his mother-in-law's seem delightful. But when it worked badly, he felt miserable, found it impossible to think his own thoughts or even to understand what he read. "Van Helmont," he thinks, "was quite right when he situated in the stomach the centre of all our affections and the active cause of our intellectual dispositions and even our ideas." This is not a piece of cheap cynicism; for never was any man less cynical than our philosopher. It is simply the statement of a fact in the life of incarnated spirits—a fact which has to be accepted, whether we like it or not, and made the best of. A great Catholic mystic has recorded his inability to place his mind in the presence of God during the half-hour which followed his principal repast. It was the same with Biran. After dinner he was generally incapable of any but the most physiologically private life. The psychologist and the metaphysician disappeared, and for an hour or two their place was taken by the mere dim consciousness of a stomach. Biran felt these humiliations profoundly and never ceased to bemoan them. His friend Ampère, on the contrary, preferred to treat his body with a slightly theatrical defiance. "You ask of my health," he writes in reply to an enquiry from Maine de Biran. "As if that were the question! Between us there can be no question but of what is eternal." Noble words! And yet all knowledge is in the knower according to the mode of the knower. Can the man who has an unsound body acquire an undistorted knowledge of the eternal? Perhaps health is not without its importance even for philosophers.

Though themselves non-historical, physiological processes can, of course, be influenced by the kind of events that are recorded in short-range, non-philosophical history books. By way of obvious example, wars and revolutions ordinarily result in famine, and famine strikes at the very roots of organic life in countless individuals. On a smaller scale, the same effects may be produced by a slump or, for certain classes of a population, by a faulty distribution of purchasing power.

As an organic experience, sex is as private and unhistorical a matter as death or sleep, digestion or sickness. As a psychological experience it may be shared to some extent by two people—not indeed completely, for no experience can be shared completely, but as much as any experience of one person can be participated in by another. *Je crois bien*, says Mallarmé.

> *Je crois bien que deux bouches n'ont bu,*
> *Ni son amant, ni ma mère,*
> *Jamais à la même Chimère.*

In the final analysis the poet is right. But fortunately analysis is rarely pushed to the limit. For the practical purposes of life, the Chimaeras which two lovers drink at one another's lips are sufficiently alike to be regarded as identical.

Social control of sex behaviour is through laws, religious precepts, ethical ideals, and codes of manners. At every period of history great organizations and a host of individuals have dedicated themselves to the task of compelling or persuading people to conform, in sexual matters, to the locally accepted norm. To what extent has this drive for conformity been successful? The evidence on which an accurate answer to this question might be based is simply not available. But such evidence as

St. Teresa

By Bernini

we have tends rather emphatically to suggest that collective efforts to make the sexual life of individuals conform to a socially acceptable pattern are seldom successful. In a minority of cases they are evidently successful enough to produce more or less severe mental conflicts, and even neuroses. But the majority go their private way without paying more than lip-service to religion and respectability.

Thus, fifty years ago, the rules of sexual decorum were much more rigid than they are today, and yet, if the Kinsey Report may be believed, the actual behaviour of men who were young at the beginning of our century was very similar to the behaviour of those who were young in its middle 'forties. Among the writers of memoirs, diaries and autobiographies few indeed have left us an honest and unvarnished account of their sexual behaviour. But if we read such all but unique documents as Jean-Jacques Bouchard's account of a seventeenth-century adolescence and youth, or as Samuel Pepys's day-by-day record of how the average sensual man comports himself a generation later, we shall be forced to the conclusion that laws and precepts, ideals and conventions have a good deal less influence on private life than most educators would care to admit. Pepys grew to manhood under the Commonwealth; Bouchard, during the revival of French Catholicism after the close of the religious wars. Both were piously brought up; both had to listen to innumerable sermons and exhortations; both were assured that sexual irregularity would lead them infallibly to hell. And each behaved like a typical case from the pages of Ellis or Ebbing or Professor Kinsey. The same enormous gulf between theory and actual behaviour is revealed by the casuists of the Counter-Reformation and, in the Middle Ages, by the denunciatory moralists and the secular tellers of tales. Modern authors sometimes write as though the literary conventions of chivalrous or Platonic love, which have appeared at various times in European history, were the reflections of an unusually refined behaviour on the part of writers and the members of their public. Again, such evidence as we have points to quite different conclusions. The fact that he was the author of all those sonnets did not prevent Petrarch from acting, in another poet's words, "as doves and sparrows do." And the man who transformed Beatrice into a heavenly principle was not only a husband and father, but also, if we may believe his first biographer—and there seems to be absolutely no reason why we should question Boccaccio's good faith or the truthfulness of his informants—a frequenter of prostitutes. Culture's relation to private life is at once more superficial, more spotty and more Pickwickian than most historians are ready to admit.

In the individual's intellectual, artistic and religious activities history plays, as we might expect, a much more considerable part than in the strictly private life of physiological processes and personal emotions. But even here we find enclaves, as it were, and Indian Reservations of the purest non-historicity. The insights and inspirations of genius are gratuitous graces, which seem to be perfectly independent of the kind of events that are described in the works of philosophical or non-philosophical historians. Certain favoured persons were as richly gifted a thousand or five thousand years ago as similarly favoured persons are today. Talent exists within a particular cultural and social framework, but itself belongs to realms outside the pales of culture and society.

At any given moment the state of the gas sets certain limits to what the creative molecules can think and do. But within those limits the performance of the exceptionally gifted is as remarkable, aesthetically speaking, at one age as another. In this context I remember a conversation between the directors of two of the world's largest and best museums. They agreed that, from the resources at their disposal, they could put on an exhibition of Art in the Dark Ages which should be as fine (within the limits imposed by the social conditions of the time) and as aesthetically significant as an exhibition of the Art of any other period. Historians have tried to find social and cultural explanations for the fact that some epochs are very rich in men of talent, others abnormally poor. And, in effect, it may be that certain environments are favourable to the development of creative gifts, while others are unfavourable. But meanwhile we must remember that every individual has his or her genes, that mating combines and recombines these genes in an indefinite number of ways, and that the chances against the kind of combination that results in a Shakespeare or a Newton are a good many millions to one. Moreover, in any game of hazard we observe that, though in the long run everything conforms to the laws of probability, in the short run there may be the most wildly improbable runs of good or bad luck. Periclean Athens, Renaissance Italy, Elizabethan England—these may be the equivalents, on the genetic plane, of those extraordinary freaks of chance which sometimes permit roulette players to break the bank. To those politically-minded people, who believe that man can be perfected from outside, and that environment can do everything, this is, of course, an intolerable conclusion. Hence Lysenko and the current Soviet attack upon reactionary, idealist Mendelo-Morganism. The issue between Soviet geneticists and the geneticists of the West is similar in essence to that which divided the Pelagians from the Augustinians. Like Helvétius and the Behaviourists, Pelagius affirmed that we are born *non pleni* (without an inherited character) and that we are affected by the sin of Adam *non propagine sed exemplo*—in our modern jargon, through social heredity rather than physical, individual heredity.

Augustine and his followers retorted that man in his nature is totally depraved, that he can do nothing by his own efforts and that salvation is only through grace. According to Soviet theory, Western geneticists are pure Augustinians. In reality they occupy a position half-way between Augustine and Pelagius. Like Augustine, they affirm that we are born with 'original sin,' not to mention 'original virtue'; but they hold, with Pelagius, that we are not wholly predestined, but can do quite a lot to help ourselves. For example, we can make it easier for gifted individuals to develop their creative talents; but we cannot, by modifying the environment, increase the number of such individuals.

Where religion is concerned, the experiences of individuals may be classified under two main heads—experiences related to home-made deities and all too human notions, feelings and imaginings about the universe; and experiences related to the primordial fact of an immanent and transcendent Spirit. Experiences of the first class have their source in history; those of the second class are non-historical. In so far as they are non-historical and immediately given, the religious experiences of all times and places resemble one another and convey a knowledge of the divine nature. In so far as they are concerned with the all too human, the home-made and the historically conditioned, the various religions of the world are dissimilar and tell us little or nothing about the primordial fact. The direct apprehension of the immanence of a transcendent Spirit is an experience of which we have records going far back in time, an experience which, it would seem, can be had by persons belonging to very primitive cultures. At what point in their development human beings became capable of this apprehension we do not know; but for practical purposes we are probably justified in saying that, at least for some persons, this apprehension is as much an immediate datum, as little conditioned by history, as the experience of a world of objects. Only the verbal descriptions of the mystical experience are historically conditioned; the experiences themselves are not. Compare, for example, the literary styles of William Law and Jacob Boehme, the first exquisitely pure, lucid and elegant, the second barbarous, obscure, crabbed in the extreme. And yet Law chose Boehme as his spiritual master—chose him because, through the verbal disguises, he could recognize a spiritual experience essentially similar to his own. Or consider our philosopher and his English contemporary, William Wordsworth. Both were 'Nature mystics,' to whom were vouchsafed ecstatic insights into the divine ground of all being. Their immediate experiences were essentially similar. We may add, I think, that they were both essentially non-historical.

In Europe, it is true, the capacity to see in the more savage aspects of Nature not only terrifying power, but also beauty, love and wisdom, is of fairly recent growth and may be regarded as being, in some measure, historically conditioned. In the Far East, on the contrary, this capacity is of very high antiquity. Moreover, Nature is not invariably savage, and at all times and in all places many persons have had no difficulty in perceiving that her more smiling aspects were manifestations of the divine. The ubiquitous cult of trees, the myths of Eden and Avalon, of Ava-iki, and the Garden of the Hesperides, are sufficient proof that 'Nature mysticism' is primordial and permanent, as unconditionally 'built-in' and non-historical as any other unchanging datum of our psycho-physical experience. Biran and Wordsworth were among those moderns who had not chosen or been compelled to close the doors of their perception. They actually saw—as all might see if they were not self-blinded or the victims of unfavourable circumstances—the divine mystery that manifests itself in Nature.

But while Wordsworth (in his youth) was a great poet, capable of creating, within the splendid tradition of English poetry, a new medium of expression as nearly adequate to ineffable experience as any expression can be, Biran at his most lyrical was merely an imitator, and an imitator merely of Jean-Jacques Rousseau. Both historically and non-historically, as inheritor of a stylistic tradition and as literary genius, he was far less well equipped than Wordsworth to tell of what he had actually perceived and understood. And yet there is no reason to suppose that his experiences at Grateloup and in the Pyrenees were intrinsically inferior to the experiences which Wordsworth had had in the Lake Country or at Tintern.

We see, then, that while every person's life is lived within a given culture and a given period of history, by no means all the experiences in that life are historically conditioned. And those which are not historically conditioned—sleep, for example, all the processes of our organic life in health or sickness, all our unmediated apprehensions of God as Spirit and of God as manifest in nature and persons—are more fundamental, more important for us in our amphibious existence between time and eternity, than those which are so conditioned.

Gas laws are entirely different from the laws governing molecules. Individuals think, feel and variably apprehend; societies do not. Men achieve their Final End in a timeless moment of conscious experience. Societies are incapable of conscious experience, and therefore can never, in the very nature of things, be 'saved' or 'delivered.' Ever since the eighteenth century many philosophers have argued, and many non-philosophers have more or less passionately believed, that Mankind will somehow be redeemed by progressive History. In his book, *Faith and History*, Dr. Reinhold Niebuhr has rightly insisted that, in itself, history is not, and cannot be, a redemptive process. But he goes on airily to dismiss the age-old revelation that man's Final End is the unitive knowledge of God here and now, at any time and in any place, and proclaims that, though history is not redemptive in any ordinary sense of the word, it is yet supremely important for salvation in some Pickwickian sense—because of the General Resurrection and the Last Judgment. "These eschatological expectations in New Testament faith, however embarrassing when taken literally, are necessary," he insists, "for a Christian interpretation of history." So far as I am able to understand him, Dr. Niebuhr seems to imply that the meaning of life will be clarified only in the future, through a history culminating in "the end of history, in which historical existence will be transfigured."

This seems to imply that all persons living in the past, present and pre-millennial future are in some sort mere means and instruments, and that their redemption depends, not upon a personal relationship, here and now, with the divine Spirit, but upon future events in which it is impossible for them to participate. Dr. Niebuhr rejects the classical and oriental conceptions of history on the ground that they reduce historical events to the "inferior realm of coming-to-be and passing away." . . . They offer no hope for the fulfilment of the unique capacities of human personality. But 'human personality' is an abstraction. In reality there are only individual personalities. Between personalities existing today and personalities existing in 3000 B.C. there is no continuity of experience. Fulfilments of persons living now are not fulfilments of persons living then; nor will fulfilments of persons living during the millennium be fulfilments of persons living in the twentieth century. Dr. Niebuhr obscures this obvious fact by speaking of societies as though they possessed the characteristics of persons. Thus "mankind will continue to 'see through a glass darkly.'" Again, 'collective organisms,' like individuals, have a "sense of the contingent and insecure character of social existence." But it is very doubtful whether a society is an organism; and it is certain that it can know nothing about the character of human existence. Individuals may make true statements about large groups; but large groups can say nothing about either individuals or themselves. Or consider the following: "Man in his individual life and in his total enterprise, moves from a limited to a more extensive expression of freedom over Nature." Here everything depends upon an ambiguity of language. By a simple trick of sentence construction "man in his individual life" is assimilated to "man in his total enterprise." But the first phrase stands for Smith and Jones, for all the Smiths and Joneses since the Ice Age, each considered as an experiencing person; the second stands for those very large groups with which actuaries, sociologists and historians are accustomed to deal. Gas laws are not the same as the laws governing molecules. What is true of large numbers is not true of individuals. From the fact that a society has achieved some measure of control over its natural environment it does not follow that the individuals who at any given moment constitute that society enjoy an analogous freedom in regard to *their* environment—an environment consisting of nature, their neighbours and their own thoughts, passions and organic processes. In the history of societies novelty is constantly emerging; but within the framework of these novelties the problems with which individuals have to deal remain fundamentally the same. The fact that one can travel in a jet plane rather than on foot does not, of itself, make the solution of those problems any easier.

"I show you sorrow," said the Buddha, "and the ending of sorrow." Sorrow is the unregenerate individual's life in time, the life of craving and aversion, pleasure and pain; organic growth and decay. The ending of sorrow is the awareness of eternity—a knowledge that liberates the knower and transfigures the temporal world of his or her experience. Every individual exists within the fields of a particular history, culture and society. Sorrow exists within all fields and can be ended within all fields. Nevertheless it remains true that some fields put more obstacles in the way of individual development and individual enlightenment than do others. Our business, as politicians and economists, is to create and maintain the social field which offers the fewest possible impediments to the ending of sorrow. It is a fact of experience that if we are led into powerful and prolonged temptations, we generally succumb. Social, political and economic reforms can accomplish only two things: improvement in the conditions of organic life, and the removal of certain temptations, to which individuals are all too apt to yield —with disastrous results for themselves and others. For example, a centralized and hierarchical organization in State or Church constitutes a standing temptation to abuse of power by the few and to subservient irresponsibility and imbecility on the part of the many. These temptations may be reduced or even eliminated by reforms aiming at the decentralization of wealth and power and the creation of a federated system of self-governing co-operatives.

Getting rid of these and other temptations by means of social reforms will not, of course, guarantee that there shall be an ending of sorrow for all individuals within the reformed society. All we can say is that in a society which does not constantly tempt individuals to behave abominably, the obstacles to personal deliverance will probably be fewer than in a society whose structure is such that men and women are all the time encouraged to indulge their worst propensities.

Of all possible fields about the worst, so far as persons are concerned, is that within which ever greater numbers of our contemporaries are being forced to live—the field of militaristic and industrialized totalitarianism. Within this field, persons are treated as means to non-personal ends. Their right to a private existence, unconditioned by history and society, is denied on principle; and whereas the older tyrannies had found it hard to make this denial universally effective, their modern counterparts, thanks to applied science and the improved techniques of inquisition and coercion, are able to translate their principles into practice on a scale and with a discriminatory precision unknown in the past.

"How small," Dr. Johnson could write two centuries ago,

> "*How small of all that human hearts endure*
> *That part which kings or laws can cause or cure!*"

In the eighteenth century it was still perfectly true that "public affairs vex no man"; that the news of a lost battle caused "no man to eat his dinner the worse"; that "when a butcher tells you that *his heart bleeds for his country*, he has, in fact, no uneasy feeling." And even in the bloody sixteenth century Montaigne "doubts if he can honestly enough confess with how very mean a sacrifice of his peace of mind and tranquillity he has lived more than half his life, whilst his country was in ruins." But the progress of technology is rapidly changing this relatively happy state of things. The modern dictator has not only the desire, but also the effective means to reduce the whole man to the mere citizen, to deprive individuals of all private life but the most rudimentarily physical, and to convert them at last into unquestioning instruments of a social organization whose ends and purposes are different from, and indeed incompatible with, the purposes and ends of personal existence.

3

The Philosopher as Moralist, Metaphysician and Candidate for Salvation

From private life in its relation to history we now turn to private life in its relation to the person who lives it, in its relation to current ethical theories, and in its relation to other private lives. For Biran the basic question in ethics was always that of freedom and responsibility. "If I were capable of regular, coherent work, I should like to investigate this problem: To what extent is the soul active? To what extent can it modify outside impressions, increase or diminish their intensity by means of the attention it chooses to pay to them? To what extent is the soul capable of controlling this attention? Such an examination, it seems to me, should precede any good treatise on morals. Before seeking to direct our affections, we should first find out what in fact is the extent of our power over them. Nowhere have I seen this matter discussed. Moralists always seem to imagine that man can give himself affections, change his tendencies, destroy his passions. According to them the soul is sovereign and can command the senses. But is this true and, if so, to what extent? And how can it come about? These are precisely the points that it would be necessary to establish."

In these lines, written at Grateloup during the Terror, Biran states a problem that was to occupy him during all the remaining years of his life. "You ought, therefore you can." Originally coined by Pelagius, the phrase had been repeated, from the height of his philosophical Sinai, by Immanuel Kant. It was a noble phrase, rousing, heart-warming. But did it correspond with the facts of experience? In the *Journal* Biran returns again and again to these questions. His answers are contradictory, because he himself is a living contradiction. At one moment he finds that he is a person who can do what he ought; at another, that he is quite a different person and cannot.

In general we may say that he is able to do the things he ought to do when those things are single acts which do not involve a prolonged struggle with his horribly capricious and changeable organism. For example, where money is concerned, Biran can almost always be as generous and self-sacrificing as he ought to be. He is charitable towards the unfortunate and, when the government is in financial difficulties, he voluntarily renounces his salary as Quaestor and accepts only his due as a deputy. Congenitally timid, he can yet, when the occasion requires, display an admirable courage. It took courage to draft the resolution presented to Napoleon by the Committee of Five; it took courage, after the Restoration, to sacrifice the esteem of the Ultras by swinging over to the moderate party. In both these instances our philosopher acquitted himself very well. His courage failed him, however, when it came to coping with his formidable sister-in-law. I suspect that the principal reason for this failure of nerve—a failure which cost his daughters their happiness and perhaps even their lives—was the fact that, with Mme. Gérard, it was not a question of doing something heroic and then grimly taking the consequences; it was a question, rather, of coming again and again to the charge, of battling with the dragon day in, day out, for weeks and months. But, for Biran, to fight this kind of battle was a physical and psychological impossibility. By the bitter experience of many preliminary skirmishes, he knew that, long before it could be won, the exhausted dragon-killer would have only one desire—to take refuge in some hiding-place, where the screeching of the termagant could no more be heard and where he might nurse his lacerated sensibilities and try to restore his impaired digestion to some semblance of health. For a victim of his own autonomic nervous system the most difficult moral problems are always those which involve 'the machine.'

For example, when his wife dies, Biran knows that he ought to accept his loss with the resignation of a Stoic philosopher. "But what can philosophy do when the soul is utterly broken, when the mind, bent under the weight of grief, has lost all its energy and activity?" With his conscious mind he can think the consolations of philosophy, he can will them to take effect. His unconscious mind pays no attention to these thoughts and his body disregards the will's commands.

It is the same with old age. According to the philosophers, who have written whole treatises on the subject, there are any number of excellent reasons why one should live out one's declining years in a cheerful contentment. But, alas, those philosophers neglected to consider "the sentiment of existence inherent in this period of life." The nature of that sentiment is such that "there is no possible consolation." What ought to be done simply cannot be done; for there are occasions—and old age is one of them—when will and reason are entirely irrelevant to the individual's actual situation. For Biran, this irrelevance of the will and reason made itself felt in another, constantly recurrent context. During the nine months of each year which he spent in Paris, Biran led the life not only of a parliamentarian and a philosopher, but also of a man about town. He dined out constantly and would go to as many as three receptions in a single evening. "There are two reasons," he says, "for going into society. Either to amuse oneself by participating in the fun, or to observe and be instructed. I do neither." Then why, why?

Year after year the question goes echoing through the Diary. He knows that philosophy is his vocation and that the life of a man about town makes it difficult, sometimes impossible, to do the work he ought to be doing, the only work that interests him. And yet, he records, "I dine out every day, indulging in deviations from my regimen; overloading my stomach and weakening my head in proportion. I have no command over myself and abandon myself to every impression. This is the way I wear out my weak and sickly remnant of a life, without any idea of the future and as though I had given up all hope of myself." For the thousandth time he resolves to turn over a new leaf, to stop going into society, to retire from politics, to settle down at Grateloup and devote himself exclusively to philosophy. But the next day he begins all over again—eating what he knows he oughtn't to eat, suffering humiliation because he feels too ill to make intelligent conversation, yet rushing from one soirée to another in a strange state of alienation and not-thereness, a state which he often compares to that of somnambulism. But though a mere sleep-walker, he retains enough self-consciousness to be intensely preoccupied with other people's opinion of him. He suffers from their indifference, craves the reassurance of their approbation and interest. He even imagines that their perfunctory compliments will make him feel as well as they say he looks. Hence an inordinate preoccupation with his appearance. If his tailor and hairdresser can make him look like a man of forty, and if somebody in a ducal drawing-room will congratulate him on his flourishing mien, perhaps he will actually *feel* like a man of forty. Or perhaps he will not. Perhaps—indeed, quite certainly—he will go on feeling like the prematurely senile man of fifty he really is. But meanwhile, he must hurry from the duke's to the minister's and from the minister's to the abbé's. And then at last he goes home.

There, alone at last and once more himself, he dips into one or other of his *livres de chevet*—Fénelon's *Letters*, the *Imitation*, the *Pensées*. "There is," Fénelon tells him (and, alas, he knows it already, knows it only too well), "there is practically nothing that men do not prefer to God. A tiresome detail of business, an occupation utterly pernicious to health, the employment of time in ways one does not dare to mention. Anything rather than God." He puts down the book, he opens his Pascal. "Man is so wretched that he would feel bored without any external cause of boredom, merely on account of his own natural condition; and withal he is so vain and feather-headed that, full as he is of a thousand reasons for being bored, the smallest trifle is enough to divert him. So that, seriously considered, man is more wretched, in that he can be amused by things so low and frivolous, than in feeling the affliction of his effective miseries, and his amusements are infinitely less reasonable than his weariness of spirit." Thanks to the style, these thoughts always have an air of incontrovertibility and self-evidence. And yet 'a reasonable boredom' is surely a contradiction in terms. Reason is incommensurable with boredom and has nothing whatever to do with distractions. "If we are bored, it is because we have an animal organization that requires constant stimulation. But this stimulation cannot be supplied by reason, or controlled by the will. It must come from without"—from those dinners, those evening parties, from all that senseless rushing from place to place.

"The bustle of social life imparts to the machine a certain state of vital activity and well-being, and this state has all the reality of an immediate experience." Biran's organism demands such immediate experiences, and demands them even though the process of getting them involves discomfort and loss of health, humiliation at the moment and shame in retrospect. The spirit is willing, is passionately desirous to lead an exclusively inward life of self-analysis and speculation; but the mind-body is weak and cannot dispense with the stimulations that come to it from outside. This fact it was "which in my youth caused me to develop a decided taste for liqueurs, which at every period of my life has made me feel the need to wind up my machine as frequently as possible."

Our philosopher's organism is addicted to society as other men's organisms are addicted to opium or alcohol. In regard to such addictions will is powerless, reason has nothing to say. "*Du sollst, denn du kannst.*" It just isn't true. And all those homilies and exhortations, all those elevating meditations and consolations of philosophy—how pointless they are, how utterly beside the mark! There is a luminous and beautifully simple world of talk, in which everything makes sense, and there is another world, obscure and labyrinthine, where men and women are condemned, or privileged, to wrestle with an unintelligible destiny.

The rational soul is often incapable of making us good. Can it at least do something to make us happy? Looking into himself, our philosopher perceives that his happiness depends, not on his will, not on his reason, but on a certain state of his psycho-physical organism. "All my thoughts and actions are directed by this condition and vary with it. Now in the most perfect calm, now in unbearable agitation, I follow all the vicissitudes of this incomprehensible state. What at one moment pains me, or fills me with joy, leaves me in other circumstances perfectly indifferent. In a word, I find I am always led by a principle of which I am not the master."

This principle is what Biran calls "the sentiment of existence." And the sentiment of existence varies according to the state of our organs and "our obscure perceptions of this state." Consequently "what are ordinarily called the buffets of fortune generally contribute much less to our anxiety and unhappiness than do the derangements, insensible because unaccompanied by pain, to which our frail machine is subject. But few are capable of studying themselves closely enough to realize this truth." And here is another illuminating generalization, derived from the facts of introspective experience. "Every individual is distinguished from all others of his species by the fundamental way in which he feels his life and in which, as a result, he feels (I will not say 'judges') his relations with his fellow beings, in so far as these promote or menace his own existence. Differences in this respect are perhaps greater than those which exist between the features of men's faces, or the conformations of their bodies. Hence it follows that it is impossible for any man completely to *know* what, as a living and sentient being, another man really is, and that it is equally impossible for him to manifest what he really is himself. . . . Only ideas resemble one another, and only ideas and the sentiments attached to them can be communicated. All that is within the sphere of our organic nature is unknowable."

We see, then, that like goodness, happiness is to a considerable extent outside the dominion of the rational soul. But the processes of thought, the world of ideas—surely these lie within its control? Once more Biran turns his eyes inwards and observes that, even when exempt from violent movements of passion, he is nevertheless by no means the master of his intellect. "Thoughts by the thousand, notions which I would like to reject, which I have not sought, which I even regard as wretchedly silly, pass through my mind. My reason sees all this, groans over it, blames or approves what is presented to it; beyond this its functions do not go. If some good sentiment arises, do you think that it is to my reason that the credit is due? No; reason confines its activity to giving its assent to what has arisen, and to doing all in its power to maintain it."

All these observations were made during, or just after, the Terror, while Biran was serving his philosophical apprenticeship, alone, among his books at Grateloup. Horrible things were happening in Paris; but the young man kept his attention firmly fixed on the events of his inner world. They were disconcerting events, and the world in which they occurred was much less tidy than his philosophical predecessors had led him to suppose; much harder to live well in than he had thought while reading Marcus Aurelius and Epictetus. For the moment he decided to do nothing in particular about the ethical problem, but to concentrate all his best efforts on the collection of psychological facts and the construction of a sound theory of human nature. The Stoics might have made some rather large and unjustifiable assumptions; but their moral system would serve very well for the time being—and perhaps if one tried hard enough and long enough, the will and the enlightened reason would actually accomplish all that the great slave and the good Emperor had said that they would accomplish. But meanwhile there was a more urgent task: to make sense of the queer, chaotic phenomena of the inner world—not the logically specious, because over-simplified, sense made by Locke and Condillac and the physiologists; not the specifically Christian sense that had been made by Pascal and the theologians; but the sort of sense that a good scientific hypothesis makes of the facts it covers. In a word, what was needed was a schematic representation of inner reality, sufficiently simplified to be comprehensible, but doing justice, nevertheless, to the essentially complex nature of the human being.

Biran's philosophy has been called a 'spiritual positivism'; and, in effect, it is based, in all its ramifications, upon carefully observed psychological facts—facts which, unlike almost all his immediate predecessors, unlike many of his contemporaries and successors, our philosopher takes as he finds them and refuses to explain away in terms of something else. For him, there is no hierarchy of facts. One datum of immediate experience is just as good as another. A fact belonging to the inner world is not less of a fact than one belonging to the outer world. "From those who explain everything in terms of sensations (Condillac and the Ideologists) to those who would have us believe that ideas, along with language, come down to us from heaven (de Bonald), the moderns have concentrated upon the outer man." How mistakenly! For "the inner man cannot manifest himself thus externally; anything in the form of image, discourse or reasoning changes his nature and, far from expressing the forms peculiar to him, completely distorts them. This is the greatest obstacle in the way of philosophy; and it may be that this obstacle is, in the very nature of things, insurmountable."

In other words, facts are always facts, wherever they may occur; but some facts cannot adequately be expressed; every representation of them in words is to some extent a falsification. And yet "such is the force of verbal habits that there is perhaps no absurdity of which one cannot convince oneself by long and frequent repetition of the signs that express it." Too often we imagine that we are empiricists, living in the world of directly experienced facts, when in fact we are the inhabitants of a home-made verbal universe, having only a rather remote connection with given reality.

Biran became conscious very early in his career of this hiatus between language and the data of experience. We shall see that, as he grew older, as his attention shifted more and more from psychological to spiritual reality the existence of this great gulf, forever fixed between words and the facts they are supposed to represent, became a matter of increasing preoccupation. Meanwhile he was concerned to establish the irreducible and primordial factuality of the inner world. The inner world, he insists, is simply there; it is a datum, a given fact which cannot be explained away. The physiologists had tried to reduce man to the stature of a merely animal and organic being; but their schematic picture of human nature was manifestly inadequate to actual experience. Or consider Locke and Condillac. If, as they had maintained, the whole of mental life were reducible in the last analysis to sensations and reflections, then "logic would be the first philosophy and indeed the whole of philosophy." But quite obviously this is not the case. As soon as one begins to look deeply into the subject, as soon as one honestly examines the facts of the inner sense, one discovers that, behind the outward man who feels, imagines, discourses, draws conclusions from premises, acts in order to satisfy his appetites and passions, carries on the business of society, tries to gain power over his fellows or to win their good opinion—behind this outward man, who is the subject matter of logical, moral and physiological philosophy, there is an "inner man who bears within him his own light, a light which is not brightened, but rather obscured, by the rays which come from without. . . . In his essence the inner man is ineffable, and within him how many degrees of depth, how many points of view have not as yet been so much as glimpsed!"

Biran did not himself undertake physiological experiments; but he was the friend of doctors and the founder of a medical society; he admired Charles Bonnet and followed the work of Bichat with the closest attention; and finally he was on intimate terms with Cabanis—the man who first used that delightfully comic phrase to the effect that "the brain secretes thought as the liver secretes bile." In spite of this extensive knowledge of the physiological science and philosophy of his time, or perhaps precisely because of this knowledge, Biran was never for a moment tempted to explain the psychic in terms of the physical. That the psychic could be profoundly affected by the physical he knew by the bitterest kind of personal experience. Bonald had pompously defined the human being as "an intelligence served by organs," *servie par des organes*. It would, said Biran, be much nearer the truth to say *asservie à des organes*. Man is an intelligence, not served by, but in servitude to his organs. But this servitude does not constitute an explanation of intelligence. "The authors of physical or physiological explanations of our sense-impressions and ideas have created for themselves the quite inconceivable illusion that by hypothetically decomposing the functions of the brain, they have analysed thought and uncovered its most secret operations." The physiologists of Biran's day made their hypothetical decomposition of brain functions in terms of 'fluids' and 'vibrating fibres.' Equipped with the most delicate and powerful electronic apparatus, their modern successors have come a great deal closer to the molecular, atomic and sub-atomic facts of cerebral activity. But the gulf between thought on the one hand and, on the other, neurones and electric charges is just as wide as that which in Biran's day divided thought from fluids and fibres.

We know that there are two orders of existence and that they are closely related. But how electrical events are converted into perceptions or abstract ideas, or how a volition becomes a nerve impulse leading to muscular activity, we do not know. Biran expressed the belief that nobody ever would know, that the hiatus between thought and matter was unbridgeable by any theory devisable by man, and must simply be accepted as a brute fact. He may have been right; on the other hand, it may some day turn out that he was wrong. In any case the ignorance prevailing at any given period of history may not legitimately be promoted to the rank of a philosophical principle.

Having established the factualness and the irreducibility of events in the inner world, Biran proceeded to their classification. Following up a hint which had been dropped by Destutt de Tracy, he distinguished between active and passive states of mind, between the awareness of a voluntary force and an organic inertia. He was delighted to find that this purely psychological classification seemed in some measure to correspond with the physiological facts revealed by Bichat in the course of his researches on the voluntary and autonomic nervous systems. "This physiological division," Biran wrote, "is consonant with that which I on my side had established between the phenomena considered from the ideological point of view."

The 'I' is not an object to be classified with other objects, but an act which we know from within, never from without. "When I say that my 'I' is a force, I am not enunciating the predicate of a subject. I am expressing the real subject as I apperceive it, or know it in itself, in its essence and quite independently of any logical predicate or accidental mode." We are directly aware of hyper-organic action upon an organic passivity, which resists it. The 'I' is this hyper-organic action which has become conscious of itself. In other words, the ego is essentially will and effort. For Descartes' *cogito* Biran substituted *volo*. "I will, therefore I am." Or, to put it more accurately and completely, "I think within myself the action of which I feel myself to be the cause; therefore I am, or I exist, in virtue of being a force or cause."

The 'I' is the self-awareness of an activity pitted against a resistance, of a free and at least potentially intelligent *providentia* at odds with brute necessity, with the givenness of an organic *fatum*. The effort by which the hyper-organic ego acts upon its *fatum* is, in Biran's words, "the type of universal causality, the model of every nexus between the two worlds of substances and forces, the notions of which rest upon the fact of consciousness and whose reality is guaranteed by the individuality and lastingness of our own being." The notion of causality is not a matter of inference; but is based upon the facts of immediate experience.

If the identity of the ego is given and can be known, the identity of the substance of the soul can only be inferred and believed. "To have self-consciousness is to exist for oneself; but to be a thing or a substance in itself is not to exist for oneself, or to feel oneself existing; for everything leads us to take the notion of being or substance in a general, universal or objective sense, as opposed to the correct and very precise meaning which the inner sense causes us to attach to the words, 'I exist.' One cannot logically proceed from knowledge of personal existence to knowledge of the substance of being; for the two belong to different logical orders—individual and universal, relative and absolute, person and thing, subject and object." But the experienced emergence of the self-conscious 'I,' as a force acting upon a resistance, imposes upon us, unavoidably and by a kind of intellectual necessity, the belief in a "virtual force, waiting to come into action." Belief in a substantial soul is forced upon us by the self-evident fact that, before there can be action, there must be being. It is legitimate, in this context, to speak of 'absolute existence.' By this term Biran means "the existence which we admit as going on in the soul, the brain, the organs, before it becomes known to the thinking being, while the latter exists only as a substance which will one day know that it exists, but which does not yet know it."

What shall we call the something which is not yet the 'I,' but which, under certain conditions, will become the 'I'? "The name is indifferent. Let it be soul, entelechy, centre, anything so long as it corresponds to a notion not only indeterminate but indeterminable by the very nature of the intellectual procedure which necessitates its existence." Our mind is under the necessity of going beyond the facts of immediate experience to the principle underlying them. "This intellectual necessity is the validation of the conclusions reached, the sufficient proof of the existence of the substance to which we are unavoidably led." The primordial fact of consciousness includes the awareness of a voluntary effort and the awareness of a resistance. "This fact necessarily has its principle in, first, the unconditional activity of a substance which we may call soul, and, second, in an absolute resistance or inertia, which we may call body." We believe in a substantial soul and a substantial body; but we do not immediately know them. For "belief in the absolute attaches itself equally to each of the two terms, when one thinks of them by abstraction; but real and positive knowledge can only attach itself to the two when united," embracing both in a single apprehension, "without separation or division."

In a word, we know ourselves as incarnate spirit, and we cannot help believing in the unconditional existence of Spirit and Matter. But so far as direct experience is concerned, these first principles are merely abstractions, of which there can be no direct intuition. "The perpetual error of German metaphysicians is to confound abstraction with intuition. . . . One must make it very clear to oneself that, wherever existence does not enter in, there can be no intuition." Our existence is always the existence of a merged duality; and our intuitions are of this duality and not of either of the two principles taken by itself.

Biran speaks disapprovingly of those metaphysicians who have attempted to reduce the experienced duality of the mind-body to some kind of unity, either spiritual or material. A true philosophy must be based upon facts; and the primordial fact of our experience is consciousness of the 'I'—in other words, consciousness of a hyper-organic activity acting upon a passive and resistant organism. "Of necessity knowledge arises through antithesis.

For man, everything is antithesis. He himself is a primitive and ineffaceable antithesis, and he forms another antithesis as against the Universe. All beings reveal themselves as antithetical in their essence—even God, whom it is impossible to conceive as a solitary being."

"Even God . . ." As a young man and during his early middle age, Biran had been, never indeed a dogmatic atheist, but profoundly an agnostic. He wished and hoped that there might be a God and was only waiting to find some compelling reason to believe that there was. "If," he wrote, "I ever find God and the true laws of the moral order, it will be by good fortune, and I shall be more credible than those who, setting out from a set of prejudices, tend merely to establish those prejudices by means of a theory." A profoundly honest man, our philosopher knew that, if one is to explore the unknown, one must not start by pretending that it is already known. If one does, that which one discovers will not be the unknown in its true objective independence, but merely a projection of one's own (or, worse, one's mother's, or one's nurse's, or one's teacher's) home-made and all too human notions about the unknown. To have a notion about a thing is never the same as being acquainted with it. Reading even the best cookery book is not equivalent to eating even the worst dinner.

As the Zen Masters like paradoxically to put it, "Buddha never taught the saving truth." Why not? Because the truth that saves is that which every individual has to realize in and for himself. The idea that saving truth can be pumped into a man from outside, by authority, is (as Biran points out in a discussion of an early and still orthodox work by Lamennais) simply preposterous. The

'I' is a hyper-organic force which is at liberty to judge what comes to it from external authority and may either accept it, or pretend to accept it, or reject it. Except in infancy, or in trance, or when exposed to reiterated suggestions, the 'I' is active and free. (Hence, of course, the zeal displayed by ecclesiastics for catching their clients young, for exposing them to the mesmerizing influences of symbols and ceremonials and for making them listen to those 'vain repetitions,' which Jesus condemned, probably because they are so horribly effective.)

Biran was a great admirer of Pascal; but he was too earnest a seeker after the Unknown God to take Pascal's advice and force himself to make those ceremonial gestures which are said to predispose the soul to faith. That sort of thing would be cheating, and Biran wanted to play the game fairly. The object of the search was the unknown. To induce in oneself, by physical means, an unfounded conviction that one already knew the unknown was most certainly not a reasonable or honest way to conduct the search.

It is significant that, even during the last six years of his life, when his primary concern was with the problems of religion, Biran hardly every spoke of faith. So far as he was concerned, faith was something irrelevant and beside the point. The point was salvation, and salvation consists in the direct knowledge or experience of God. To believe in a thing is radically different from knowing it. Moreover, a belief which is based upon authority, on somebody else's account of what may, or may not, have been a direct experience, is very often not an aid to redemptive knowledge, but actually an impediment. Almost everyone has had occasion to discover that a preconceived idea about some unmet person, or some hitherto unvisited place, may interfere with the normal process of getting to know the place or person when the opportunity of acquaintance finally presents itself. *Mutatis mutandis*, it is the same with God. If we start out with preconceived notions about God, we are likely to find that these home-made and second-hand ideas will make it very hard for us to have a direct and unmediated knowledge of the divine nature.

In religion, as in science, experience is conditioned only by itself. If we think we know the unknown for which we are looking, the chances are that we shall discover only a projection of the ideas with which we set out upon our search. For Biran the great men of the age of Louis XIV seemed enviable because they held a set of beliefs which they did not question. He saw very clearly that these beliefs were an incomparable source of strength. But he never imagined that they were a source of true knowledge; nor did it ever occur to him that he himself should cultivate their beliefs. It was not strength that he desired, but a knowledge of the hitherto unknown God, and such knowledge cannot come except to those who are pure not only in heart, but also in the intellect. It is not to the knowing, but to the unknowing, mind that the Unknown presents itself as it really is.

This fact is clearly recognized by the Christian mystics, who find themselves in the embarrassing position of having to forget, every time they make a near approach to the primordial fact, most of the articles of their faith. These home-made and second-hand notions are found not to correspond with immediate experience. If these notions are retained, there will be no experience and the believer will suffer a great and perhaps irreparable loss. If the experience is preferred and the notions are rejected, even momentarily, then it must become clear to the believer, if he uses his reason, that his beliefs are not quite so important as he had been led to suppose. They may fortify and console, they may permit him to construct coherent pictures of the universe (*credo ut intelligam*); but they are not means to that knowledge of God, which is salvation.

Our philosopher was an agnostic who wanted to become a gnostic. So far as knowledge was concerned, faith seemed useless. Could logical reasoning be of any help? Biran examined the various proofs of God's existence and found that they proved the existence of nothing except the words of which they consisted. Nor was he convinced by the moral argument: God exists, because virtue exists; and virtue can have no other source or sanction than an all-good God. "But in all sincerity," Biran confides to his Diary during the Terror, "I can affirm that, when I do good, I never in fact think about God." If our philosopher behaved as well as he did, it was only because he saw that vice is ugly and destructive, and that virtue is intrinsically beautiful and will make us happy. In a word, to live well is merely reasonable. But delete the qualifying adverb, and what then? Simply to live, to have existence—what has reason to say about that? "The man who lives, who thinks and who does not lean on God for his support, can only shudder, amazed and appalled, at feeling himself exist. If God is not, why are we? Why is there anything?"

Like Pascal, Biran lived in the presence of an abyss. What made him dizzy was not the silence of the interstellar void (to which he never paid any attention), but the buzzing and pullulating fullness of consciousness. Strange to the point of inconceivability, and yet a brute fact of immediate experience. In order to become intelligible or even tolerable, this gulf of multitudinous noise seemed to require the existence of an infinite Silence. But did that Silence exist? And, if so, how was it to be discovered? In the hope of an answer, Biran turned to the records of traditional religion. "The religious and moral beliefs which reason does not make, but which are reason's basis and necessary starting-point, now appear to me as my only refuge, and it is precisely there where in the past I could see, with the *philosophes*, only dreams and illusions that today I find true knowledge."

Written in 1815, this passage seems to assert that our philosopher had already found what he was looking for. Over-optimistically, he often thought that he had reached his destination; but a little later it would always turn out that he had been wrong. There were always new reasons for reconsidering conclusions, for questioning apparent certainties, for yet once more suspending judgment. He may have ceased to believe, with the *philosophes*, that religious and moral beliefs were illusions; but he could not yet feel certain that they were substantially true.

In the writings of his maturity, Biran applied to the problem of God's existence the same arguments as he had applied to the problem of the existence of substance. We are not immediately aware of the substance of our soul or our body, but the nature of our mind is such that we are under an intellectual necessity to believe in them. It is the same with God. Our mind is under the necessity of proceeding from immediate knowledge of an 'I,' in relation to a passive not-I, to belief in a substantial soul, and from this belief to belief in an unconditioned Being underlying and giving support to the substantial soul. Beliefs, as Biran defines the word, are personal and individual, but for that very reason universal; for the 'I' is the same in all men to the extent that all men are under the same intellectual necessities. "Deprive notions of their personal character, and you have nothing left but abstractions, mere artificial collections, or the symbols of such collections. Instead of real beings expressed by their real names, you will have the great Collective Whole, or the one Supreme Cause of all that is." Moreover, belief in God is an intellectual necessity only to the man who looks inwards. "The elements of all knowledge, including the most important of all, the notions of cause, belong to the inner world and have no analogy with the elements of the outer world, sensations and images. To derive the idea of God from a contemplation of the order of external phenomena is to draw water from the wrong well. In this way one reaches, not the living God, but the God of Spinoza. The personality of God can be understood only as the type of the personality of the 'I'; and this can be known only by immediate inner apperception."

God may, and indeed must, be believed in. Can He also be known? Biran's answer, in these middle years of his career, was that God is not an immediate fact of the inner sense. Indeed, He cannot be; for "the fact of personal causality is the first datum of all real knowledge and admits no idea of a cause above it." Our dependence upon God is not a datum; it is an inference from a necessary belief. The 'I' cannot know God directly; nevertheless, belief is often supplemented by a kind of indirect knowledge, through feeling. "Sentiment is the mediator between human thought and the infinite."

From this brief summary of a few of the principal features of the Biranian system, as it was elaborated in the years between 1794 and 1818, we must return again to the man and his actual experiences. As he grew older —and he aged prematurely—Maine de Biran found himself ever more helplessly the victim of his machine. In his various treatises he had clearly demonstrated the inadequacy of a philosophy of human nature, based upon the notion that the mind is wholly passive and the mere creation of its sensations.

But the knowledge that he was theoretically right could not console him for the immediate experience of being physically and morally wrong. He felt that he was a failure. He was tormented by the thought that he had betrayed his vocation, that he had been sent into the world to do something, but had done nothing. To future historians of philosophy he would be known as the man who, in the teeth of Condillac and the Ideologists, had re-habilitated the hyper-organic 'I'; to himself, he was the man whose 'I' was forever being defeated by his organism. "*J'assiste à ma mort avec les forces entières de ma vie.*"

Even as a young man, in the full flower of such strength as he had ever possessed, Biran had his doubts about the ethics of Stoicism. But he had chosen to put these doubts aside and, provisionally at least, to accept Marcus Aurelius and Epictetus as his guides. This acceptance was more than merely passive. On more than one occasion

Biran went out of his way to uphold the Stoic doctrine of the sufficiency of will and reason against the Christian teaching that will must be supplemented by grace and reasoning by inspiration.

But our philosopher was an empiricist who (unlike some of his fellows) was always ready, when a new fact presented itself, to modify his theories in such a way that they would "save the appearances." For the ageing Biran, the fact of "being led by a principle of which he was not the master" was by no means new. It was a fact, of which he had taken note in 1794, but from which he had so far refrained from drawing any conclusions. By the second Restoration it had recurred so frequently and, in spite of all his efforts to be a Stoic, so insistently, so overwhelmingly, that it was no longer possible to pretend that it could be eliminated or explained away. It had now to be admitted that, all too frequently, organic inertia was stronger than hyper-organic force. And, not content with mere passive resistance, the body and the unconscious mind would often counter-attack, routing the forces of will and reason and hunting them ignominiously from the field. On these occasions our philosopher would be as a man possessed, powerless to do anything but look on, while the usurping demon who bore his name and wore his elegantly old-fashioned clothes, deliberately compromised his highest interests and forced him to play the fool.

Biran admitted the existence of the unconscious mind, but attributed all its malice, its madness and its imbecilities to its 'obscure perceptions' of untoward events taking place within the body. It never seems to have occurred to him that, in some cases at least, the perversity of his organic *fatum* might be the effect of strictly psychological causes; that his present miseries might be due in part to his reactions to forgotten, or deliberately ignored, events in the past; and that the bodily sickness which so adversely affected his mind might itself have been aggravated by a mental disturbance of which the 'I' was now completely unaware.

In this context, a special significance attaches to the rather odd and surprising fact that Biran, in his *Journal*, almost never speaks about his childhood or his parents. He mentions his father and mother only once, and then only to remark that he has inherited from them certain traits of physique and temperament, certain idiosyncrasies of behaviour, which he wishes he didn't have. The single reference to his childhood goes back no further than his fourteenth or fifteenth year—a time when he used to be "recollected, tender, wholly occupied with the inward impressions which were then dominant," but have since given place to the adult's "frivolity and lack of feeling." In a psychologist who was the father of three children, who had studied Pestalozzi, founded schools and was the president of a semi-official committee on Elementary Education, this all but total indifference to his own childhood and the influences which had formed his character is perplexing in the extreme. Biran himself offers no hint of explanation, nor do his biographers, who tell us, presumably because they have been able to discover, absolutely nothing of what happened to our philosopher as a child and, later, a schoolboy. We may guess, I think, that Biran's early years were uneventful, that he was not particularly fond of either of his parents and, except to the sister whose death is the subject of one of his earliest essays, was little attached to the other members of his family. If he neglected to study his own early history, it was probably because his memories of it were neither rapturous nor excruciating, and so did not compel his attention. Moreover, throughout his adult life, he was always so busy on the introspective analysis of present events that he could give no serious thought to what had happened to him in the past.

Biran was an empiricist, but an empiricist within a limited field. The facts upon which his system is based are exclusively the facts of adult experience. He analyses his psychic life as he finds it, by introspection, here and now; and he takes no account of the fact that what he is here and now may be, to a considerable extent, the result of what he was, what he did, what he thought, willed and felt during a much earlier and more primitive period of his personal history. Biran's is a static psychology based upon the minute analysis of a number of cross-sections of adult experience. The notion that personality is something that cannot be completely known except as a process in time does not seem to have occurred to him. Neither did it occur to his contemporaries. Dynamic and biographical psychology is a comparatively recent invention. Culture is, among other things, a negative force—a something which prevents persons, living in certain places and at certain times, from being able to think certain thoughts or adopt certain styles of expression. The culture of Biran's time and place was such that psychologists found it very hard to think of the human being historically, as a development in time. And the culture of our own age is such that it is very hard for psychologists, who have no difficulty in thinking historically, to see the developing personality-in-time against the background of eternity.[1]

Biran, then, was largely ignorant of the psychological, as opposed to the physical, determinants of his recalcitrant *fatum*. But of that recalcitrance he was acutely aware. Prolonged and most unhappy experience convinced him at last that the Stoics were wrong, that will and reason were not sufficient and that the individual could not, unaided, live as he ought to live, much less be 'saved,' or 'illumined,' or 'made perfect.' His 'I' knew that it needed the help of some benevolent not-I more powerful than itself. And such help was actually forthcoming. The insufficiency of the 'I' was a matter of immediate experience; but so also was grace, so was inspiration. "Communication of the Spirit with our spirit is a true psychological fact and not a mere matter of faith."

Again, "men are fortified by inspiration, or the belief in inspiration. A man who does not put his trust in some higher power and who does not open himself up to inspiration, is doomed to be a mere cipher in the eyes of others as well as in his own."

And here is what he writes on a spring day in 1816. The weather has suddenly changed for the better. "I feel another man. . . . In the air one breathes at this season of the year there is *something spiritual*, *which seems to draw the soul towards another region*, and to give it a strength sufficient to overcome all organic resistances." Gone are the obstacles placed by a malign *fatum* in the way of moral virtue and intellectual lucidity. "It is not my ideas that grow clearer—a thing which ordinarily happens when I

[1] See, in this context, the valuable study by Dr. Hubert Benoit, *Métaphysique et Psychanalyse* (Paris. 1949).

fix my attention and apply my active faculties; it is my *inner light* that becomes brighter and more striking, so that the heart and mind are suddenly illumined by it. I have often detected in myself these sudden and spontaneous illuminations, when the truth emerges from behind a cloud; it seems that our material organization, which was the obstacle in the way of inward intuition, ceases to be resistant and that the spirit has nothing to do but receive the light which is appropriate to it."

These experiences make him wonder if the will has any real action upon our ideas or inward perceptions. He is inclined to think that the most it can accomplish is to "repress the influence of the organism and in this way to remove the hindrances that block our intuitions." In another entry, Biran tentatively answers his own question. "To judge by what I experience . . . it seems to me that there is within me a superior sense, and as it were a face of my soul which at certain moments turns itself towards an order of things or ideas superior to all that pertains to common life, all that binds us to the interests of this world. I then have the inward feeling, the true suggestion of certain truths having reference to an invisible Order, a mode of existence better and wholly other than that which is ordinarily ours."

The same theme is more fully developed in the following remarkable passage. "If I consult my own experience I have in all honesty to confess that all my good impulses and thoughts have always depended upon certain organic conditions as foreign to my personal activity as digestion, nutrition, growth, illnesses and all the changes in my feeling of existence, which in their turn depend on the seasons of the year, the temperature and all the rest. . . .

There is a force independent of the will which modifies us in spite of ourselves, and upon which depends our happiness or unhappiness. . . . Is this force blind and devoid of purpose? In that case it is the *fatum* of the body, the animal instinct, the principle of life recognized by the physiologists as being subject to the laws of medicine and hygiene. Is it intelligent and sovereign throughout nature? In that case it is God, whose effective action follows the laws of grace. On either hand we find impenetrable mysteries and insoluble questions—for the so-called solutions are wholly in the field of logic. Whether God acts directly upon our souls, or whether He acts upon the organization and the affections of the vital principle so as to produce upon the soul the sentiments and ideas corresponding to changes in the body, the fact remains that in all cases it is the whole man who thinks, wills, acts, feels his existence, and not the soul in isolation. . . . Certain bodily states produce good dispositions of the mind. Sometimes these dispositions have led me towards God; they were not for the body, though they came from the body. We depend on our physical organization for the higher light which illumines our minds and permits us to enjoy the truth, just as we depend on the sound conformation of our eyes to see the light of the sun."

To sum up, the hyper-organic 'I' is aware not only of a resistance within the organic not-I, but also of an assistance. Moreover, the not-I is not exclusively organic; there is also an indwelling light which is seen to be as much beyond the merely hyper-organic as the hyper-organic is beyond the merely organic. These facts had been forcing themselves upon Biran's attention for half a lifetime. But it was not until after 1818 that he finally made an attempt to bring his spiritual life and his metaphysical theories into harmony with the data of his immediate experience.

But before we examine what Biran actually did and thought during the last years of his life, it seems worth while to consider certain things that he might have done, but actually did not do, certain thoughts which he did not think, but which, if he had, would have found a place ready and waiting for them in his system. I will not apologize for the digression; for, as I have said before, what a philosopher leaves unthought, along with the reasons for this omission, may be no less illuminating than his actual thinking.

Let us begin with a few reflections on Maine de Biran's attitude toward the arts. From his biographers and from his Diary we learn, or guess, that painting and sculpture left our philosopher completely indifferent.

Once, under the Empire, he went with a party of friends to visit David's studio. That was as near as he ever came to the plastic arts. In literature he was more at home. He was familiar with the best classical authors and, as a young man, he had written bad verses and been a worshipper of Rousseau. But the art he loved most was music. He was a fair performer on violin, harp and keyboard instruments, and in the years spent in Paris before and during the Revolution, he played constantly and with delight. Indeed, his delight was so intense that he felt it necessary, when he embarked upon his philosophical career, to give up the practice of music almost completely. Music, he found, acted too strongly upon his sensibilities. To Saul, the sound of the harp brought peace; to Biran it brought an emotional and nervous agitation not at all conducive to philosophic reflection.

In this context it is interesting to read what Biran has to say (in a paper on *Obscure Perceptions* read before the Medical Society of Bergerac) on the effects of musical timbre. Quite independently of the words sung or the music played, the timbre of certain voices and instruments has the power to "rouse or calm the various passions, sometimes to heal and at other times to produce certain nervous disorders. I myself have witnessed the extraordinary effects produced by the sweet and melancholy tones of the Harmonica." (This curious instrument—generally known in England as 'the Musical Glasses'—was perfected by Benjamin Franklin, enjoyed a fleeting but prodigious popularity during the later years of the eighteenth century and then, almost overnight, vanished so completely that, when a modern virtuoso wishes to play the ravishing harmonica music composed by Mozart, he must be content, for lack of Musical Glasses, with a mere *Glockenspiel.*) "I have seen persons," Biran goes on, "too sensitive to be able to resist the effect, persons who, at the first impressions of those sounds, shuddered in every part of their body, then burst into tears and finally fell into a swoon."

That Biran himself ever actually swooned, seems unlikely; but we can feel pretty sure that he shuddered and perhaps occasionally wept. For he belonged to that not inconsiderable class of persons who love music, not wisely, but too well—love it sensually and viscerally, with their nerves, their solar plexus, their palpitating heart and yearning bowels. Because of their excessive sensibility, such persons cannot see the wood for the trees—cannot hear the music for the noise. They are so completely intoxicated by their immediate sensations that it is impossible for them to pay attention to the artistic whole, of which the intoxicating sounds are the constituents. The combination of, say, clarinet with strings, of harpsichord with *viola da gamba*, is intrinsically delicious. Whether the music produced by the happy concord of these instruments is good or bad is a question which, for these voluptuaries of sound, hardly arises. From the references to music scattered throughout his *Journal*, it is evident that our philosopher never asked himself this question. Music, for him, is simply a pleasure—self-forbidden just because it is a pleasure and distracts him from his philosophical labours.

In 1815 he comes away from the Opera, feeling sadly that he is too old for music, that he has lost his taste for any kind of pleasure. His relish for sound is purely physiological; it belongs to the organic not-I and is so imperious, so mind-eclipsing, that it prevents him from understanding that works such as *Don Giovanni* or *Orfeo* give not only pleasure, but a great deal more beside. Biran's curious inability to hear anything in music but the delightful noise is betrayed by the fact that, though he frequently makes mention in his Diary of concerts and operas, he only once records the name of a composer. Thus at one soirée he hears "a duet for harp and horn"; at another, where "the music and the company are both first-rate," M. Garat-Faby "sings admirably"; at a third, given by the Minister of Police, there is "a fine concert." But a concert of what? And what did Garat-Faby sing? And who wrote the duet for harp and horn? We are left completely in the dark. On only one occasion is the music named and attributed to an author. In December 1820, he goes to hear Rossini's *The Barber of Seville*. At the theatre he finds himself in a box next to that of Pozzo di Borgo, the Corsican who had become a Russian and was now the Tsar's ambassador to France. Biran is so "transported by the fine music" that he "ventures to talk with the ambassador in a more open and animated way than he had done at other times about the change of ministry and the position of the new ministers in relation to the Chamber."

In a word, the fine music excited him to the point where he loses his shyness and can open his heart to a foreign diplomat about domestic politics. Once again we see that, for our philosopher, art is merely a stimulant, a something that "winds up the machine." It is experienced as a fact that primarily concerns the *fatum*, not the hyper-organic 'I,' still less the divine not-I, which transcends the ego and is its ground.

For George Herbert—a man who physically and temperamentally was very close to our philosopher—music was a permissible pleasure, inasmuch as it seemed to give the soul a foretaste of the joys of heaven. In other words, the aesthetic experience is in some sort an analogue of the mystical experience. By coming to know perfection in a work of art, we gain a kind of knowledge of the ultimate nature of things. Art is one of the means whereby man seeks to redeem a life which is experienced as chaotic, senseless and largely evil. By itself, art can never be completely redemptive. It can only point in the direction from which redemption comes; it can only indicate at one remove the nature of the primordial and ineffable Fact. *Don Giovanni* is about a man who, in Spain alone, seduced one thousand and three women, and it tells the story of this man consummately well. Yet the total effect of the opera is to "give us a foretaste of heaven."

That Biran had at least some theoretical notion of the significance of art may be inferred from an entry in the *Journal*, in which he professes himself to be thoroughly persuaded that "without virtue there is no true genius. And if one sometimes meets with lofty minds accompanied by vile souls, the reason is that such men lose their baseness in the instant of starting to write, and that, for a few moments, genius elevates the soul. The vicious man is not the same as the man who writes; in the act of writing he has forgotten his true nature."

This passage implies a belief in the reality of artistic inspiration and a conviction that, as well as giving pleasure, art effects a temporary transfiguration and illumination of the soul. But this adumbration of a theory of art was based on no immediate experience, and for this reason, presumably, was never fully developed. The fact seems all the more astonishing when we reflect, first, that Biran was an existentialist, who insisted that man must always be considered as he really is, an incarnate spirit or mind-body, and, second, that art is manifestly, among many other things, a kind of 'spiritual exercise,' by means of which the incarnate spirit can advance towards redemption. His failure to give art its proper due must be attributed, I think, to physical causes altogether beyond his control. He was a chronically sick man, who had to suffer endlessly from the vagaries of 'the machine.' In the inseparable 'duumvirate,' as he liked to call his mind-body, the second constituent was a 'body of this death'; and for this reason he was constantly tempted to pass from existentialism to Platonism, from an acceptance of life as it really is to a longing for a life completely 'spiritualized' by the elimination of Brother Ass.

This Platonizing propensity reveals itself in what our philosopher says about beauty. "Strange that all which is beautiful, grand, perfect, everything truly harmonious and unified, exists only in man's mind, has no archetype in external objects and indeed cannot be realized apart from man! In Nature there is no model of perfect beauty and no perfectly regular figure." In a philosopher who had insisted that we must always think of man in his wholeness, as he really exists, this association of perfection with the abstract seems strangely inconsistent. Pure geometry and the *beau idéal* are symptoms of the weakness of minds which cannot grasp life as it is, in the concreteness of individual existence, and which therefore arbitrarily abstract from reality only those elements which are amenable to logical treatment.

Biran, unfortunately, had never read Meister Eckhart. If he had, he would have known that "my inner man relishes things, not as creatures, but as the gift of God; but to my innermost man, they savour, not of God's gift, but of ever and aye." Interpreted in aesthetic terms, this means that, whereas the spiritualizing Platonist finds perfect beauty only in the Ideas which are supposed to fill the mind of a mathematical God, the mystical existentialist finds it in concrete things; for he perceives the divine in every creature and the external in every moment of time. In this and other instances, Biran's inconsistencies were imposed upon him by his yearning to be rid of the burden of an ailing body. "'Few,' writes the author of the *Imitation*, 'become better through illness.' I am habitually ill; in consequence I feel myself profoundly incapable, and am far from becoming better."

That Biran could have thought so little about art, and with such a lack of his ordinary subtlety and penetration, is strange but, in view of his excessive sensibility and his chronic ill-health, comprehensible. Much less easy to explain is his neglect of a subject which he had ample opportunities of investigating at first hand, and from the study of which he might have learned many things of the utmost importance to a metaphysician of the inner life. I refer to what, in our philosopher's day, was called 'animal magnetism.'

Like every intelligent Frenchman of his time, Biran was well acquainted with the facts and fictions of animal magnetism, with the excessive claims of its proponents and the wholesale denials of the medically orthodox. He had studied the record and he agreed with his eminently judicious friend, Cuvier, that some at least of the effects of mesmerism were real. He knew that many people had been cured by animal magnetism of their diseases. He considered it probable that there was "in all living organisms a more or less marked power to act at a distance and exercise an influence outside themselves within a certain sphere of activity, analogous to the atmosphere that surrounds the planets."

He accepted extra-sensory perception as a reality and considered that "those who deny such communication between persons, or between a soul and a higher spiritual power, have a very narrow and materialistic view of the faculties of the soul." The fact that minds could communicate with one another directly, without making use of their physical organs, seemed to make the facts of grace and inspiration a little more comprehensible. "Prayer," he wrote near the end of his life, "is turning the eyes towards the light; effort creates the conditions which make it possible for light to penetrate the soul. In the words of a greatly gifted woman of my acquaintance, 'Prayer is the magnetism of the soul.'"

To anyone who accepted the reality of the principal phenomena of the mesmeric trance—healing, clairvoyance, and thought transference—it must have been very evident that, for a psychologist and metaphysician of the inner life, the whole subject of animal magnetism was one of capital importance. And yet, after writing a youthful memoir on Somnambulism, our philosopher chose to do almost nothing about it. And this in spite of the fact that, after 1818, he was on terms of personal friendship with two eminent magnetists: Sébastien de Planta, a Voltairean converted by the study of mesmerism to a kind of theosophical Catholicism; and J. P. F. Deleuze, librarian of the Museum of Natural History, translator of Erasmus Darwin, author of the standard history of animal magnetism and himself a veteran magnetic healer and investigator, with an unblemished reputation for moral integrity and scientific accuracy. So far as we know, Biran never made use of the opportunities which these friendships placed within his reach. He never made magnetic experiments on others, and he never submitted to any on his own person. And yet, if he had done the first, he would very quickly have discovered that the problem which had baffled him all his life was in certain circumstances actually soluble—that there were means whereby organic resistance could sometimes be overcome, whereby the sub-personal not-I could be made to obey the commands, first of an alien 'I' and then, as hetero-suggestion gave power to auto-suggestion, of its own hyper-organic self.

And if he had permitted the second, if he had allowed himself to be mesmerized by an experienced operator such as Deleuze, it is more than possible that this victim of psycho-somatic illness might have been almost miraculously cured of many of his most distressing symptoms. We know at any rate that, some few years later, Harriet Martineau, who suffered from a more excruciating form of our philosopher's chronic indigestion, was, after five years of painful and, medically speaking, incurable sickness, completely restored to health by four months of magnetic treatment.

What were the reasons for Biran's neglect of a subject possessing, for a spiritual positivist, such profound significance? Could it be that he was put off by the name, 'animal magnetism,' and the physical or physiological theories with which Mesmer had tried, and most of his successors, were still trying, to explain the phenomena of trance, healing and extra-sensory perception? In Biran's day the wilder spirits still spoke of a cosmic force, akin to magnetism or electricity, which the operator could somehow concentrate and direct. The more cautious, like Cuvier, contented themselves with a mere transfer of nervous energy across the gap that separated the operator's fingers from his patient's head or body. In either case something physical, something fluidic or vibratory, was involved.

Because of this something physical behind and beneath the psychological phenomena, certain enthusiastic magnetists, such as Elliotson, H. G. Atkinson and

Harriet Martineau, felt themselves justified in professing a thorough-going materialism that culminated in philosophic atheism. (In later life, Dr. Elliotson graduated from mesmerism to table-turning, and from spiritualism to Christianity. Miss Martineau stuck to her magnetic guns to the bitter end.)

That our philosopher should have wished to steer clear of this revived physiologism is very comprehensible. But meanwhile there was, quite obviously, nothing to prevent him from studying the psychological phenomena without reference to the theory which sought to explain them in terms of cosmic forces or nervous fluids. Alexandre Bertrand had already done precisely this, and even Deleuze, who believed in the magnetic fluid, had the good sense to be inconsistent and to speak, whenever it suited him, a purely psychological language. Biran must have known very well that the investigator of animal magnetism was committed neither to animals nor to magnets, but could, if he chose, do his work without reference to physics or physiology and within a frame of reference exclusively psychological.

Clearly, then, our philosopher's failure to seize the golden opportunities provided by Deleuze and Planta was due to something more than a distaste for the name and a disbelief in the current theory of this new branch of psychological science. We shall not, I think, go far wrong if we attribute it to a combination of causes, constitutional, temperamental and intellectual. To begin with, he was, at the epoch of his intimacy with Deleuze and Planta, a prematurely old man, too sick and too tired to undertake the new and arduous business of psychological experimentation. But Deleuze was a veteran therapist, and being cured by him would have involved no effort. Alas, Biran was too touchily over-sensitive to submit to being made the *corpus vile* of someone else's experiments, too secretively the introvert, too inhibitedly cerebrotonic, to be willing to take the risk of 'giving himself away.' For a man of his temperament, being experimented on, even for his own good, was practically out of the question. And for a psychologist, who had been driven by this same temperament to reject behaviourism and adopt a purely introspective approach to his subject, so was experimentation on others. Even as a young and relatively healthy man, Biran had never chosen to look for light outside the confines of his own mind.

And finally, there was a cogent intellectual reason for our philosopher's neglect of animal magnetism. He was a metaphysician of the inner life; but the introspection upon which he relied for the data of his philosophic system could reveal only a fragment of that life. Outside the little circle of light was a vast dark universe in which organic resistances and repressed memories played the part of monsters, but where (as he was now coming to realize) there were also good angels in the form of graces and inspirations having their origins at every level from the purely physiological to the spiritual and perhaps the divine. In magnetic trance considerable areas of this hidden world beyond the ken of introspection were plainly revealed, and others could be guessed at. But Biran had spent half a lifetime refuting Condillac's sensationism. Again and again, as he pronounced the word *moi*, his pointing fingers had touched his own breast, symbolically attesting the reality of the hyper-organic 'I.' But if animal magnetism had any lesson to teach, it was that the hyper-organic 'I' is less important in the total human economy than it likes to think. Through direct experience, interpreted in terms of Christian mysticism, Biran had come, in these last years of his life, to an essentially similar conclusion, and in the *Nouveaux Essais d'Anthropologie* he meant to bring his philosophy into harmony with these conclusions, by incorporating it, with a few necessary modifications, into the Platonic-Christian framework of the three lives, animal, human and spiritual.

A study of mesmerism might have enlightened him as to the way in which the three lives are connected and act upon one another. But since time was short—so short, indeed, that the *New Essays* were never more than adumbrated—Biran preferred to concentrate all his energies on thinking out the problem within the ancient and hallowed frame of reference provided by classical philosophy and Christian spirituality. If the 'I' had to surrender some of its proud claims, let it be to Plato and Fénelon rather than to Mesmer, Puységur and Deleuze. And let the surrender be purely voluntary and self-suggested, not imposed from without by a study of other 'I's.'

Biran's almost pathological reluctance to look into any mind but his own caused him to miss another golden opportunity for increasing his knowledge of inspiration and the gratuitous graces. For years his closest friend had been the elder Ampère, and Ampère was that almost unique phenomenon, a man of all-round genius who had started life as a 'calculating boy.' When a child, who has not yet learned the rules of arithmetic, solves in his head and almost instantaneously complicated problems which would cost an intelligent and highly trained adult hours of wearisome labour, who is it that accomplishes the feat? Certainly not the infant 'I' and certainly not the organic resistance to that hyper-organic force. Somebody else is at work. But who, and where, and how? So far as one can discover, Biran never put these questions to his friend; nor did Ampère ever propound them as a subject worthy of philosophical discussion.

In this matter their younger contemporary, Sir John Herschel, saw further and more clearly than they. Herschel possessed the curious faculty of seeing, while fully awake, 'geometrical spectres,' which "obtruded themselves on his notice and, by calling attention to themselves, directed the train of thought into a channel it would not have taken of itself. . . . If it be true that the conception of a regular geometrical pattern implies the exercise of thought and intelligence, it would almost seem that in such cases we have evidence of a thought, an intelligence, working within our own organization, distinct from that of our own personality."

The infant Ampère's prodigies of calculation were instances even more striking of the workings of an intelligence within the organization and yet distinct from the personality. For a philosopher who had spent his best energies in establishing the reality of the hyper-organic personality, and who was now wrestling with the problems of grace and inspiration, the opportunity to study an intelligent not-I at first hand was not to be missed. But in fact it *was* missed, and missed even more completely than the opportunity to study the intelligent not-I as it manifests itself in the magnetic trance. With Deleuze and Planta, Biran at least talked about these problems. In his discussions with Ampère they were not even mentioned.

Biran was by no means the only philosopher to ignore the subject of animal magnetism. "I should doubt," wrote F. W. H. Myers more than half a century ago, "whether there have been a hundred men in all countries together, at the ordinary level of professional intelligence, who during the century since Mesmer have treated hypnotism as the serious study of their lives." The great majority of philosophers have not treated hypnotism and the allied phenomena of healing and extra-sensory perception as the serious study of a year or even a semester. And yet if they had looked into the matter, if they had examined the masses of carefully sifted evidence accumulated by such scientific organizations as the Society for Psychical Research, they would have found themselves confronted with strange data very hard to explain in terms of the philosophic systems recently current in the West. A natural reluctance to give up deeply rooted intellectual habits coupled with the disreputableness of a subject that had attracted more charlatans than serious investigators, sufficiently accounts for the fact that most modern philosophers have chosen to go about their business as though hypnotism and its related phenomena were simply non-existent.

That they will be able for much longer to preserve the virginity of their voluntary ignorance seems unlikely. Up till now the story of hypnotism has been a record of alternating ups and downs, of periods of popularity followed by periods of neglect. In the eighteen-twenties Deleuze felt quite certain that magnetic therapy was destined very shortly to become a branch of orthodox medicine; his German contemporaries shared his conviction, and so did his English successors of the 'thirties and 'forties. All were wrong. From a note appended by the American translator to the sixth chapter of Deleuze's text-book we learn that "probably there is not a city nor village in North America where there could not be found at this time—1878—one or more magnetizers; usually one can be found in every family." A few years later they were all gone. In the last years of the nineteenth and the first of the twentieth century there was a certain revival of interest in the subject. But Freud disparaged the therapeutic value of hypnotism, and it is only recently that psychiatrists have begun once more to make extensive use of it as an adjutant of analysis. But meanwhile the soldiers and the policemen and the politicians have discovered its possibilities. In a recently published volume C. H. Estabrooks has described some of those possibilities. To the horrors outlined in his chapter on 'Hypnotism in Warfare' must be added the psychological atrocities which are being perpetrated in the prisons of the police states. So far these methods have been used for the extraction of confessions. But, skilfully employed, hypnotism can do much more than this. By its means the dictator can modify the expression of his subjects' personality, can compel their idolatrous devotion to the State and Party, can invade and almost abolish their private life, can make them love their slavery. And if these methods, along with those of childhood conditioning and life-long suggestion, can serve the purposes of totalitarian dictatorship, it is virtually certain that they will be used, and used on an ever-increasing scale.

At the same time we may expect to see in the West an increasing concern with the techniques of *yoga*. The spiritual exercises of India and the Far East will be scientifically studied, improved and then applied (as the Nazis seem to have applied them in their Schools for Leaders, as the Japanese militarists applied them in the training of officers) for the purpose of achieving purely mundane and even diabolic ends. The corruption of the best is always the worst. We have come to our present plight by concentrating too exclusively on externals, but our present plight will seem paradisal by comparison with the state we shall be in after concentrating, for a generation or two, on psychology, particularly at its deeper levels. In a certain sense it was perhaps fortunate that nineteenth-century philosophers and men of science should have paid so little attention to animal magnetism. Because they refrained from investigating the facts or working out an explanatory theory, there was no 'pure science' of psychology for such all too practical men as soldiers, politicians and policemen to apply. Thanks to nineteenth-century materialism on the one hand and, on the other, to nineteenth-century idealism and respectability, the date of the third and final revolution was postponed for more than a century.

We have had political revolutions and economic revolutions. Nominally for the benefit of the masses, these revolutions have resulted in the concentration of power in a few hands; and the maintenance and increase of this concentration of power have tended to become their main purpose. But economic and political power is, by those who exercise it, never felt to be enough. Tyrants cannot be satisfied until they wield direct psychological and physiological power. The third revolution is that which will subvert the individual in the depths of his organic and hyper-organic being, is that which will bring his body, his mind, his whole private life directly under the control of the ruling oligarchy.

Sixteen years ago, when I wrote *Brave New World*, I fancied that the third revolution was still five or six centuries away. Today that estimate seems to me excessive. Mr. Orwell's forecast in *Nineteen Eighty-Four* was made from a vantage point considerably further down the descending spiral of modern history than mine, and is probably more nearly correct. It may be indeed that he is completely right and that, only thirty-five years from now, the third revolution, whose crude beginnings are already visible, will be an accomplished fact—the most important and the most terrible fact in human history.

Meanwhile we are still happily at liberty to discuss the purely philosophical implications of animal magnetism. What, we may still ask, are the conclusions, to which a serious study of those tabooed phenomena may be expected to lead? The question may best be answered by a statement of what in fact has been thought by some of the few men, in Biran's day and in our own, who have chosen to recognize their importance for philosophy.

By profession Deleuze was not a philosopher, but a naturalist and scholar, who during more than half of a long life devoted all his leisure to the gratuitous healing of the sick by the methods of animal magnetism. He developed no metaphysical system and, since he was a Catholic, felt no need to do so; but here and there in his historical and practical writings he sometimes states the metaphysical conclusions which the observed facts have forced upon his mind. Thus, he is convinced that "though it generally makes use of the sense organs, the soul can in certain states receive ideas and sensations without the mediation of these organs." And he adds that "this principle once recognized, the strongest argument, nay, the only argument, against the immortality of the soul is destroyed."

Another interesting conclusion is that all human beings possess within themselves "a torch and a compass." At ordinary times the distractions of worldly life and their native egotism prevent them from being illumined by the inner light or guided by inspiration. But torch and compass are always there, ready and waiting to serve their appointed purpose.

Deleuze draws this conclusion from his observations of a rare somnambulistic state in which the hypnotized person seems to be in a kind of contemplation or *samadhi* that alternates between rapt silence and the utterance of sublime things. "Happy the man," says Deleuze, "who has chanced to meet a somnambulist of this kind! For there is no means of bringing forth from an ordinary somnambulist the faculties just described." He adds that the state would probably occur more frequently if magnetizers were less frivolously curious, less eager to prove their own preconceived theories and more ready to allow the sub-conscious mind of the patient to go its own way.

From Deleuze we turn to another of Biran's contemporaries, a man whom our philosopher never knew and whose works he could not read. The fact is unfortunate; for, in spite of all his eccentricities, Franz von Baader was a profound and original thinker, in whose discussions of the problems of religion Biran might have found many new and profitable ideas. Like most of those who participated in his country's Romantic Movement, Baader was passionately interested in animal magnetism, and, above all, in the phenomena of extra-sensory perception by which the magnetic trance was sometimes accompanied. He read, and too easily believed, all the contemporary accounts of magnetic marvels and himself carried out experiments on entranced subjects. The metaphysical conclusions which he drew from his findings were set forth in several short treatises on magnetic ecstasy and divination, and took their place as integral constituents of his philosophy.[1]

Baader was of the opinion that 'magnetic ecstasy' is a temporary disembodiment and unbinding of the psyche, "a state in which the aggregate of body, soul and spirit, which is our personality," is reduced to pure consciousness. Waking trance is superior to normal waking, inasmuch as "in the magnetic state consciousness acquires a broader and deeper foundation." The knowledge we have during trance is 'disorganized,' in the sense that it is unmediated knowledge, which does not come to us through the bodily organs. In Baader's curious terminology it is 'magical knowledge,' or knowledge within the sphere of the Magical, which may be defined as the state in which Idea has not yet been realized, not yet undergone the transformation into act.

Ecstasy is of two kinds—a downward ecstasy into coma and catalepsy, and an upward ecstasy into the Magical and beyond the Magical into the Spiritual. The first is an anticipation of death, the second of the state described by theologians as that of glory and resurrection. In upward ecstasy man returns to the condition he was in before the Fall. He ceases to be the egocentric

[1] See *Franz von Baader et le Romantisme Mystique*, by Eugène Susini (Paris, 1942), especially Vol. II, Book IV, Part 2, Chapter V.

parody of himself and becomes for a moment *tel qu'en Lui-même enfin l'Eternité le change.*

Between death and magnetic ecstasy there is a difference, not of kind, but only of degree. "If," says Baader, "one reflects that these ecstatic states are more or less anticipations of death, one can easily understand the disquieting impression produced by their occurrence on the average normal and healthy man, endowed with what is called common sense." It is for this same reason that the normal man finds it so hard to conceive such phenomena, that he displays such a strenuous will to disbelieve them. He voluntarily ignores them because, if he did not, they would bewilder and appal him in the same way that physical death bewilders and appals him.

Baader was a Romantic and a Theosophist—in the sense, of course, in which that word was used before the apparition of Mme. Blavatsky. These appellations cannot be applied either to Dr. C. D. Broad or to Professor H. H. Price; but these two eminent modern philosophers resemble their German predecessor in at least one respect: they have taken account, when writing about man and his place in the universe, of the facts of parapsychology. Having examined the evidence for foreknowledge and telepathy and having found it provisionally convincing, Dr. Broad has shown what must be the nature of a time dimension, in which future events are predictable, and has argued that the 'psychic factors' of human personalities must bathe, so to speak, in a psychic medium, out of which they have crystallized, through which they are interconnected and within which they may for a time survive the death of the body.

Like Dr. Broad, Professor Price accepts the evidence

for parapsychology. If, he argues,[1] the phenomena of extra-sensory perception and psycho-kinesis are facts, then it is impossible to go on believing in that Cartesian world-picture which has been accepted so long and so universally that, in the West at least, it now seems mere common sense. Descartes divided the universe into matter, having extension as its essence, and into separate, substantial minds, having consciousness as their essence and interacting with the matter in their own body, but not directly with other matter or with other minds. Cartesianism must be dropped and a philosophy more consonant with the facts must take its place. According to this philosophy man would be a tripartite being, composed of body, mind (the 'soul' or 'psyche' of earlier philosophers) and 'spirit' (a word which is used by Professor Price as equivalent to "the pure ego, the *Atman* of the Hindu philosophers"). Minds, as distinct from spirit or *Atman*, are "the subject matter of psychical research and of all the psychological sciences," and minds, in spite of Descartes, are not indivisible entities, are not separate from one another, are not necessarily incapable of interacting with all matter except that in their own body and do not have consciousness as their essence. On the contrary, minds carry on many, perhaps most, of their activities on the sub-conscious or unconscious level; they may, and if the evidence for psycho-kinesis and telepathy is sound, they actually do act directly upon other minds and upon matter outside their respective bodies; and they are not persistent substances, for such unity as they possess is "precarious and unstable."

[1] See his article, "Mind Over Mind and Mind Over Matter," in *Enquiry*, July 1949.

A philosophical theory capable of 'saving the appearances' must take as its primary unit, "not a mind, as Descartes did, but what I shall call an *idea*." Ideas are the ultimate elements of the mental world and from these elements are built up all kinds of psychological entities "from ghosts and Freudian complexes at one end to the healthily integrated waking human mind at the other." (It is interesting to translate these notions into the language of Buddhist philosophy. According to this philosophy, the human being is *anatta*, without a substantial and permanent soul and is composed of *skandhas*, or complexes of sub-personal psychic elements.)

Professor Price assumes that all ideas have their origin in some individual mind. Perhaps he is right; or perhaps, as Biran and von Baader would certainly have maintained, some ideas arise from sources that are not originally human. In any case "once an idea has come into existence it has, so to speak, an independent life of its own." Some ideas exist only for a short time, some outlive the body associated with the mind that has them. They may exist and be operative in an individual consciousness, or in an individual sub-conscious or unconscious, or perhaps in the no-man's-land of the psychic medium. All ideas have an inherent tendency to realize themselves in some concrete physical form. Some may achieve only a symbolic realization in somebody's imagination. Others may get as far as producing a quasi-public hallucination or apparition. Others may succeed in getting themselves completely embodied through the instrumentality of a nervous system and a body. And if we accept the evidence for psycho-kinesis, we must suppose that an idea sometimes "succeeds in materializing itself in a physical object or event without making use of somebody's brain or muscle."

The familiar sequence of idea, nervous impulse, muscular activity and embodiment of idea in matter or event is only a particular case of the general tendency of ideas to embody themselves at any price and by fair means or foul, normally or paranormally. "You will observe with suitable horror," says Professor Price, "that this is just one of the fundamental assumptions of primitive magic. I cannot help it; perhaps primitive magic has a little grain of sense in it, after all." And he adds that the more respectable activity of petitionary prayer seems to be based on the same assumption. "The fact that prayer sometimes works does not, of course, compel us to accept the theological theory of how it works."

So much for the conclusions which our philosopher might have drawn from a study of animal magnetism and the phenomena of trance, but which he did not draw because he chose to neglect his opportunities for study. From the facts which he *did* choose to observe—the facts of his own inner experience—he drew a set of conclusions which, in many important respects, are similar to those reached by his German contemporary and his English successor. In other respects his picture of the mind in its relation to the universe is dissimilar to, and less satisfactory, than theirs. This inadequacy is due to Biran's exclusive reliance on introspection; for ordinary introspection is, by its very nature, incapable of yielding any knowledge of the sub-conscious and unconscious states which can only be inferred from overt behaviour or, if they manifest themselves in trance, can only be observed from outside. That most of the mind's activities go on beneath the level of consciousness; that the soul (as distinct from the pure ego, or *Atman*) is not a separate substance, but a not too clearly defined aggregate of psychic elements connected with, or even overlapping, other aggregates; that there is, in Baaderian language, a realm of the Magical, in which ideas clamour and fight for physical realization and that this realization can take place not merely through a particular nervous and muscular system, but in other ways as well—such thoughts are, by an exclusively introspective philosopher, hardly thinkable, because the facts which suggest them are hardly within his ken.

In the fragments of the *Nouveaux Essais d'Anthropologie*, Biran sketched the outlines of the general system, into which he hoped to incorporate, and in terms of which he meant to interpret, all his previous findings. "Man," he wrote at the beginning of this, his last, unfinished work, "is intermediate between God and Nature. He belongs to God by his spirit and to Nature by his senses. He can identify himself with the latter by allowing his 'I,' his personality, his liberty to be absorbed in his senses, and by giving himself up to all his appetites, all the urges of the flesh. He can also, up to a certain point, identify himself with God, by allowing his 'I' to be absorbed through the exercise of a higher faculty, which the school of Aristotle completely misunderstood, which Platonism distinguished and characterized, and which Christianity perfected by bringing it back to its true archetype."

Up to this time our philosopher had spent most of his energies on the task of establishing the existence of the hyper-organic 'I,' and of defining its relations with the organic not-I and external Nature. In the *New Essays* he

Monument to Maria Camilla Pallavicino

By G. Mazzuoli

would have another task: to show how Nature, Organism and 'I' are related to the Spirit, and through the Spirit to the divine not-I which transcends, and is immanent in, all things, all lives and all minds.

The world picture into which Maine de Biran now proposed to fit his psychology and his metaphysics of the inner sense was ancient, grand and majestically simple. Perhaps, indeed, it was a little too majestically simple to be fully adequate to a world of immeasurable complexity or to the life in that world of an amphibious being made up of contradictions and incongruities—a life that modulates continuously from the tragic to the farcical, from the absurd to the divine, from the unintelligibility of necessity to the unintelligibility of grace.

In philosophy, Biran was an existentialist, who knew that man is an incarnate spirit and that it is as an incarnate spirit that he must live and, if possible, be 'saved,' 'liberated,' 'illumined.' But the machine was feeble, Brother Ass irremediably spavined. Hence, for Biran, a standing temptation, that grew stronger as his infirmities multiplied upon him, to retreat from existentialism into a Platonism that equated good with disembodied spirit and evil with matter. Direct experiences of ecstatic detachment from the organism and a second-hand knowledge of some of the phenomena of mystical and magnetic trance tended to confirm him in this Platonic view of things, to make him think of the problems of life in terms of a dualism of mind and matter, and not in terms of the normal datum of experience mind-matter or incarnation. More Christian than our philosopher ever was, and better acquainted with the facts of magnetism and the literature of theosophy and mysticism, Baader was ready to admit that body, soul and spirit were not inseparable, that they formed an aggregate rather than a completely unified whole; but he insisted that, in this present life, their dissociation was abnormal, that it could not be persisted in without danger and that salvation must be achieved by the aggregate for the aggregate. In theory, and if he had remained consistent with his earlier self, Biran would have agreed with Baader. In practice, as we learn from his Diary during the last years of his life, he found it very difficult not to be a Platonic dualist. When, as he not infrequently did, he experienced a state of what the mystics would call 'sensible consolation,' he was always tormented by the thought that it might have been due to some happy accident within his body, some casual concordance of organs with one another and with the hyperorganic force. The tacit assumption was that, if this were the case, his mystical (or, to be more accurate, his premystical) experiences would not be genuine, would not come from God and would not, in so far as they were cognitive, have any reference to the divine nature.

In a Platonist this *a priori* mistrust of the body is right and reasonable. But an existentialist cannot harbour it without being unfaithful to his first principles. To him it is self-evident that, in very many cases, grace *must* be organically mediated. And he knows, by observation and experience, that there are animal graces which are primarily for the body, and that there are also animal graces which, through the body, are primarily for the mind and spirit. At the same time he infers that there must be, and observes in practice that there are, graces of the mind, intellectual, imaginative, emotional—graces that in some instances are indirectly helpful to the body and that, in others, assist the mind to make itself aware of the spirit. And finally, he knows that there must be, and are, purely spiritual graces, which come when there is a temporary dissociation of the three elements of the human aggregate, and that these spiritual graces are at the same time graces for the mind and the body.

But always there were those disturbing questions. "If magnetism were to produce the same state as that which the mystics reach in the prayer of silence, would not that be a proof that there is a physical element in all these supernatural states?" May not the beatitude, experienced as the result of self-abandonment to the divine will, be related "to some state of the affective sensibility such that, if the organic disposition were to undergo a change, all this inward calm, this heavenly blessedness, would vanish, leaving in the soul nothing but trouble and confusion?" And those sensible consolations which come to him, unsought and of their own accord—"are they of organic origin, or induced by the imagination, or infused by grace? To assure oneself of the reality of one or other of these causes of mystic sentiments is to my mind the greatest and hardest problem of the science of man."

And yet, so long as the human aggregate persists, one cause can never be exclusive of the others; the beatitude which follows self-abandonment, and even the act of self-abandonment itself, must be related to, and conditioned by, certain dispositions of the organs; and in most 'supernatural states' there is bound to be a physical element—which means that there must be appropriate psycho-physical methods for creating the conditions most favourable to such states.

Because they are closely knit aggregates rather than completely unified and indissoluble wholes, human beings are capable in some degree of temporary self-transcendence and can therefore come to at least a partial knowledge of the transcendent Spirit. But during most of their existence it is impossible for them to be aware of Spirit except as immanent in themselves and in the minds and lives and things outside them. Divine immanence is possible only because there is divine transcendence. There can be no indwelling of one piece of matter within another piece of matter; and, though they may overlap, minds can never fuse, never wholly possess one another. But Spirit, which is of another order of being, can be completely co-extensive with bodies, co-active and co-conscious with minds. For this reason the realm of nature is always, potentially, the realm of grace. For the potentiality of grace to become actual, or for an actualized gratuitous grace to become permanently effective, there must, of course, be collaboration by the will.

The sick body is rarely in a state of animal grace, and its gracelessness, as Biran knew by the most bitter experience, may make it very hard for even the most passionately aspiring 'I' to achieve union with the spiritual not-I. And yet sickness, as Biran had also discovered, may turn the mind inwards upon itself and so make it aware, however obscurely and remotely, of the existence and the infinite desirability of that not-I. The healthy body, on the other hand, lives so continuously in a state of animal grace that its 'I' unreflectingly takes this condition for granted and uses the physical energies, made available by health, to multiply distractions until they raise a barrier between itself and the divine not-I even more insurmountable than that created by sickness. The Good Fairy, with her precious gifts, is always potentially the Bad Fairy, who lays a curse upon the cradle.

In the philosophy and practice of any genuinely spiritual religion the significant and decisive dualism is not the Platonic dualism of body and mind, but the mystics' dualism of time and eternity. Mystics belonging to all the great religious traditions have affirmed that salvation is possible here and now, and that it consists in the redemption of time by eternity, the transfiguration, within an individual life, of temporal events and experiences by a moment-to-moment awareness of their timeless ground and eternal significance.

"Time," says Meister Eckhart, "is what keeps the light from reaching us. There is no greater obstacle to God than time"—or, to be more accurate, than the time-obsessed consciousness which lives in memory and anticipation rather than in the timeless now. Eckhart, in another place, quotes the words of St. Paul, "Rejoice in God all the time," and adds that "he rejoices all the time who rejoices above time and free from time. Three things prevent a man from knowing God. The first is time, the second is corporality, the third is multiplicity. That God may come in, these things must go out—except you have them in a higher and better way: multitude summed up to one within you."

In other words, the Platonic dualism with its practical corollary of escape from the body, through ecstasy or death, into pure spirituality is admissible; but salvation is complete only when time, body and manifoldness are accepted and transfigured through being apprehended in their relation to eternity. When a man so apprehends them, he can maintain, as Eckhart maintained, "that I already possess all that is granted to me in eternity. For God in the fullness of His Godhead dwells eternally in His image, the soul," and it is, so to speak, with the eyes of God that the soul is now looking at the world. The mind-body dualists are tempted to break out of what they regard as their prison and to sink themselves completely in what they believe to be the One.

But, in the Buddhist terminology of Huang-Po, "when senses and thoughts are annihilated, all the passages to Universal Mind are blocked." Universal Mind is to be recognized in sense-impressions and thoughts, not as belonging to them, nor yet as independent of them. The true philosophy and the right conduct of life cannot, of course, be based on an unreflecting acceptance of what the sense organs and the discursive reason have to tell us. But at the same time "you must not seek Universal Mind apart from sense and thoughts. Do not try to grasp Reality by rejecting your senses and thoughts. When you are neither attached to them, nor detached from them, then you enjoy freedom and enlightenment." For free and enlightened beings, the external world is no longer what it was for our philosopher, "a world of necessity, in which man is carried away like all the other objects of nature, towards a goal of which he is ignorant, by a series of means which he neither feels nor controls, or which he can feel without being able to control." It is the world which many children inhabit, the world whose loveliness has been expressed (with what incomparable power!) by Wordsworth and Traherne. In that transfigured other-world, which is yet our world, "eternity is manifested in the light of day and something infinite behind everything appears, which talks with my expectation and moves my desire."

Peter Sterry was another who lived in that world. "Didst thou," he asks, "ever descry a glorious eternity in a winged moment of time? Didst thou ever see a bright infinity in the narrow point of an object? Then thou knowest what Spirit is—the spire-top whither all things ascend harmoniously, where they meet and sit contented in an unfathomed Depth of Life."

Such, then, is the mystical conception of true and complete salvation, a conception of which, strangely enough, Biran seems hardly to have been aware. Notwithstanding his growing concern with the subject, he had, so far as we can discover, read very little in the literature of mysticism. Though he might have known them, or at least have known about them, we find in his *Journal* no reference to Eckhart or Tauler, to Ruysbroeck or St. John of the Cross, to Boehme, Law or Saint-Martin. With the relevant Oriental literature there was, of course, in Biran's time practically no possibility of acquaintance. In the *Nouveaux Essais*, it is true, we meet with a reference to the book, in which Abel de Rémusat, the first man to occupy a chair of Chinese in any European university, had maintained that the Logos of Pythagoras and Plato was identical with the Tao of Lao-tsze. That is as near as our philosopher ever came to the spiritual positivism of his Oriental predecessors. With the mystical tradition of the West, Biran's main literary link was Fénelon, the Fénelon, above all, of the *Spiritual Letters*. But though unrivalled as a psychologist, teacher and casuist of the spiritual life, Fénelon lacked the passion for metaphysical speculation and was not himself overwhelmingly a mystic.

The immediate insights and the theoretical constructions of the great philosopher-contemplatives were beyond his scope. To the extent that Biran had chosen to depend, for his knowledge of mysticism, upon Fénelon (together with Fénelon's old enemy, Bossuet), he was debarred from a knowledge of what those philosopher-contemplatives had written.

What he did not learn from books our philosopher might, of course, have discovered on his own account. But, as we have seen, his constitution, his temperament and his circumstances conspired to make that discovery exceedingly difficult. His chronically ailing machine almost forced him to equate evil with matter and good with a purely spiritual state of disembodiment. His excessive sensibility caused him to react to music so physiologically, so gluttonously and voluptuously, that it was all but impossible for him to think of art except as a source of mere pleasure. That it might be used as a means for redeeming the squalid chaos of human life, that the aesthetic experience might be an analogue of the mystical experience, bringing with it insight as well as rapture—such ideas did not, perhaps could not, occur to him.

And finally there was Nature. As a boy, as a young man, he had sometimes seen "eternity manifested in the light of day and something infinite behind everything." But then he had become a professional politician and a professional philosopher, dividing his time between the statistical and the abstract, between the merely institutional in the outside world and the merely personal and organic in the world of introspection. And meanwhile he needed constant stimulation, he had to be forever "winding up his machine," lest he should fall into melancholy and a kind of hebephrenic lassitude. Hence his addiction to dinner parties and soirées, to those diversions of high society which he found at once indispensable and unutterably boring, shameful and necessary, tonic and yet utterly destructive to health and happiness. And these diversions could be had only in Paris, far from the nature he had loved and felt himself a part of and apprehended as a manifestation of the divine. Because he was, congenitally, who he was, because of his body, his mind, his character, because of his profession and his social commitments, Biran was destined never to discover the true nature of mystical salvation.

But salvation was what he was looking for; freedom from the burden of his selfhood and a lightening of his darkness were the things he craved. It was easy enough to frame a philosophical system based upon the idea of man's tripartite nature as animal, mind and spirit; and it would not be too difficult to fit his own earlier writings into this half-Christian, half-Platonic framework. As always, as for everybody, it was only in practice, only in relation to the concrete facts of existence that there was any real difficulty.

Anybody with the requisite wits and learning can write philosophy; the problem is to *be* a philosopher or lover of wisdom. Kant, Hegel, Schopenhauer, Nietzsche, to name the first that come to mind—all wrote, but none of them *was*. "A man may stand very high in the intellectual scale, and yet be in complete opposition to the spirit. Pride, self-centredness, attachment to his own particular notions may fill his mind with continual agitations and anxieties." And again: "In my study I think like a spiritual man, outside I behave like a carnal man." From thought to intention, from intention to will, and from will to action and conduct, the road is not smooth, nor even continuous.

With the problem of the will there went, in Biran's mind, the problem of cognition. It was easy enough, if one knew the jargon, the talk about the ultimate nature of things, easy enough on hearsay, or authority, or as the result of specious reasoning from not too closely examined premises, to profess to know something about God. The difficulty, once again, was to pass from theory to practice, from talk to experience, from a superficial and indirect knowledge about to an immediate and concrete acquaintance with.

After 1818 Biran sought a solution to these two problems in the more or less regular practice of prayer. Not, of course, petitionary prayer; for Biran was in search of salvation and enlightenment, and the asking of favours is in no way redeeming, since it makes the petitioner aware, not of the Unknown, the immanent and transcendent Spirit, but merely and yet once more of his own all too familiar wishes. What he refers to in the Diary is always the prayer of meditative silence, the prayer of self-emptying and waiting. Sometimes he can report "a day of well-being, reason and tranquillity, the effects of prayer." More often he complains that he has no disposition for prayer and that, lacking all desire and facility, he has neglected to pray and lost the habit of it. As usual, it was the law of his members at odds with the law of his mind. He knew what ought to be done, but he could not do it. "The presence of God makes itself felt by an inward state of calm and elevation, which it is not in my power either to initiate or maintain, but which might become more habitual thanks to an intellectual and moral regimen, to which it is high time that I should submit myself by the prayer of silence and recollection." It was high time; but still the submission was only partial and spasmodic.

In its essence nothing could be simpler than the prayer of silence. But since human beings are in their nature manifold and successive, nothing is harder for them than to enter a state of essential simplicity. Biran often neglected to pray, and when he remembered or was able to try, his attempts to silence his mind and organism, and to wait recollectedly for the coming of the divine not-I, were very often unsuccessful, and he would find himself, not contemplating God, but doing yet again the thing he had done innumerable times before—he would find himself peering, with a mixture of self-satisfaction and disgust, at the workings of his own mind.

As a younger man, he had been proud of his introversion, had thought of it as a secret and unrevealed title of honour, which placed him, for all his outward inferiority, on a level far above that of the hereditary or self-made bigwigs among whom he moved. Ministers, peers of France, diplomats, men of affairs, all the riff-raff of court and senate and drawing-room and counting-house—in their company he felt like a whipped dog; but at the same time how he despised them! Rich and powerful, they ruled a world in which, with their strong muscles or their big bellies, their extraversion of force or of facile geniality, they were perfectly at home. But he, the scrawny and intimidated fop, the voiceless parliamentarian, the disregarded philosopher, of whom a Third

Consul had said (how truly!) that he would never be good for anything, he was the discoverer and monarch of a world infinitely superior to theirs—the inner world, the world of the mind.

Nosce teipsum. By being an introspective psychologist he was obeying the commands of the philosophers. And not only of the philosophers, of the saints as well. All the masters of the spiritual life were agreed that the first, indispensable step on the road to perfection was to transform the mind into a *cell of self-knowledge.* In a word, the candidate for salvation must be recollected. But "observation in psychology is identical with recollection." Better still, to think about these observations is a peculiarly meritorious form of right action. For "speculation is an exercise of morality; there can be no truly moral beings except those who speculate and so raise themselves above the world of the senses." The introverted thinker is not merely justified, he is exalted above his fellows.

And then, almost suddenly, a doubt crept into our philosopher's mind. This habit of continual introspection —was it, after all, a thing to be proud of? Did it really make him superior to the extraverts? "I have been," he says, "the prey of strong and disorderly affections; and instead of trying to resist the tendency to be carried away by them, I let myself go without effort, taking pleasure in observing the impulses and judging their effects, as I might do in regard to someone else—or as a doctor might congratulate himself upon contracting some disease, because this gives him an opportunity of observing it in his own person. . . . This habit of paying minute attention to what is going on within oneself—

is it perhaps immoral? My experience makes me fear that it is. One must give oneself a goal and a fulcrum outside and above oneself. Only in this way can one react successfully to one's own modifications, even while observing and analysing them." Introspection for its own sake, introspection that fails to go beyond the 'I' and the organism, tends inevitably to transform the active conscience into a merely speculative conscience. The habitual introvert is liable to become primarily scientific when he ought to be primarily moral, to think only of facts in situations where he should be thinking of values.

But this is by no means the only danger of introspection. Biran came to be convinced that "the germ of the spiritual life is always present in the depths of the soul." But he also knew that, above those depths, "the soul finds in itself only imperfections, vilenesses, miseries, vice and frivolity." Such moral and religious truths as we know have a source that is "different from that of the truths of psychology, which are limited to man as a sensitive, free and independent being and depend, as Kant has rightly recognized, upon other faculties." Introspection is the process by which the 'I' becomes aware of itself and the organic not-I—becomes aware, that is to say, mainly of "imperfections, vilenesses, miseries" and all the rest. The divine not-I lies beyond these products of hyper-organic force and organic resistance, beyond even its own manifestations in good intentions, true insights and rapturous states of 'sensible consolation.' It is something which can be known only when the soul is intently abandoned, alertly passive. This condition is a paradox in action, and the words which describe it seem to contain a contradiction in terms. It cannot be otherwise, for our existence is intrinsically contradictory and paradoxical. From the muscular to the spiritual, from sport to contemplation, in all life's workings above the merely physiological, the results we desire are obtained only when we contrive to combine will with effortlessness, action with relaxation. Soul and body must let go; for only thus can they make themselves receptive to animal graces from the realms of the instinctive and the physiological, to intellectual and imaginative graces from the lower levels of the psyche, and to spiritual graces, whose source is beyond those depths in the divine immanence. They must let go; but at the same time they must not completely let go—for the 'I' must use its will to bring itself and its body into the condition which, at each successive moment, is most favourable to the influx of animal, mental or spiritual grace. Towards the end of his life, our philosopher understood very clearly the nature of life's fundamental paradox. "It has occurred to me that the activity which causes the soul to be present to itself and constitutes it a person, or ego, in its own eyes, has been given to it for the sole purpose of raising itself above its sensible nature and directing that nature towards a moral and spiritual end. The 'I' creates nothing, except the animation or feeling which accompanies it; as for the ideas and conceptions which are present to it, these are beheld by a light which is intimately connected with it but which it does not create, a light which is within it, but which is not identical with itself. This is that 'true light which lighteth every man that cometh into the world,' this too it is which is *Deus in nobis*, God in us." In other words, the highest function of the personal will is freely to will itself out of existence, so that the divine will may be done, and done not only on the intellectual and spiritual level, as Biran here suggests, but also (an idea which was not too acceptable to a Platonist with an ailing body) on the physiological level, by making possible an irruption of animal grace. "Impose silence on yourself and allow the spirit of God to speak and act in you." But it was a great deal easier to copy these words of Fénelon's into the Diary than to act upon them during his times of meditation. One cannot "impose silence" on oneself, for there is a "Law of Reversed Effort," and the act of imposing silence increases the inward noise. "The soul's bane," says our philosopher, "is not suffering, but agitation. Agitation is doubly an affliction—for it is an affliction which the will rejects and, in rejecting, intensifies."

The introvert's prayer of silence modulates with a fatal facility into self-observation; and self-observation, even if its purpose be strictly scientific and philosophical, is, in relation to the Spirit, an agitating experience. And if one attempts to suppress this agitation, one merely increases it. The way to silence is not, as it would be logical to suppose, through the imposition of silence; paradoxically as always, it is through an acceptance of noise. If an attempted prayer of silence turns into mere self-observation, self-observation is the fact of immediate experience which must be accepted. It must, however, be accepted neither as a means to wish-fulfilments and the compensations of imagination and memory, nor even as a means to a scientific classification of facts and the establishment of a philosophic theory; it must be accepted as it is, without preconceptions and without the intention of doing anything with it, accepted passively, and yet alertly, in an act of quasi-aesthetic contemplation which permits the facts to be seen not as they are in relation to the wishing and theorizing 'I,' but as illumined by the inner light. For it is the light that will impose silence and calm an agitation which the will and the intellect can only increase.

The active introspection, which starts from a set of preconceptions and which aims at some specific achievement, is not identical with recollection, and the self-knowledge in which it results neither enlightens nor redeems. Redemptive self-knowledge comes when the 'I' breaks out of its home-made and second-hand frame of reference and is thus enabled to see itself freshly, from moment to moment, in that light which it finds, but does not create. As always happens, when we leave the sphere of the all too human, we find ourselves in the midst of paradoxes and impossibilities. In order to live effectively in the world, we are compelled to do most of our thinking in terms of the home-made and the second-hand. In order to achieve salvation and enlightenment, we must rely, at each instant, upon insight coming from the divine not-I, by whom we are inhabited. On one level it is *cogito*, on the other, *cogitor*. Here the 'I' thinks; there it is thought. Here the hyper-organic force is active and independent; there, when at last it finds itself in harmony with divine immanence, its state, in our philosopher's words, is a "kind of sublime passion, which has this advantage over other passions that, for it, all evils are changed into goods." The contradiction would seem to be irreconcilable—but only logically, only in theory. In living practice it is possible for the mind to pass very rapidly from one level to the other, or even to exist

The Tomb of Pope Urban VIII

By Bernini

simultaneously on both levels, so that it preserves a measure of insight even when relying on its home-made notions, of spontaneity even when making use of the second-hand.

Maine de Biran had an inkling of what it was to go beyond himself to the divine not-I—but no more than an inkling. His sick body and, above all, his lifelong habit of thinking about the self were too strong for him. Except on the rarest occasions, it was impossible for him to forget his 'frail machine,' or to relax the ego's possessive hold on everything that concerned itself. He knew that the light was there, and sometimes he could actually see it. But though he longed for it, he could not prevent himself from turning his back to it and looking at other things. "I am," he wrote in 1820, "and I have always been the most personal man that can be imagined. It is an instinct that irresistibly impels me inwards, forcing me to pay attention to everything that is of immediate concern, materially or intellectually, to myself. In my first youth I was preoccupied with my face, with all my externals, all the inward and outward affections pertaining to the organism and to sensuous appearances. Later on I was dominated by my concern with the operations of my own mind. I gave all my attention to its behaviour and its modifications just as, in the past, I had given all my attention to my face and the means of charming others or of pleasing myself by reflection from the outside. But in the eyes of his fellows as in the eyes of God, a man has worth only in so far as his constant and immediate goal is not himself, but lies beyond himself."

During the four years that remained to him, Biran came only a very little nearer to this goal beyond himself. In 1824, a few months only before his death, we find him lamenting that, though he has lost all taste for the things of this world, he has acquired no taste for the things of the spirit. The light is always present; but it was in an enforced night of sickness, in the God-eclipsing contemplation of a self for which he could now feel only disgust, that he found himself advancing towards the final and most strictly private event of his career. On the last page of his Diary we read a passage from the Book of Job: "*Cunctis diebus, quibus nunc milito, expecto donec veniat immutatio mea.*" All he could now do was to imitate the prophet and "wait in patience until the great change shall come about."

Seven weeks later, on his death-bed, Maine de Biran returned to the fold in which he had been brought up. After having lived first as an agnostic, then as a would-be gnostic, a seeker of a direct experience of the divine, our philosopher ended as a believer. He was dying, he needed support, and belief, as he had remarked long before, is the great source of strength. Whether it does, or can, lead the believer to that knowledge of God in which alone, to use the words of the Anglican Prayer Book, "standeth our eternal life," is another question.

ART AND RELIGION

DOES art hold up the mirror to its period? Or does every period hold up the mirror to its art?

Does the artist follow or lead? Or does he walk alone, heeding only the categorical imperatives of his talent and the inner logic of the tradition within which he works?

Is he the representative of his epoch? Or does he stand for a constituency no wider than that particular class of talented persons—his predecessors, contemporaries and successors—to which, by the predestination of his heredity, he happens to belong?

All these questions can be correctly answered now in the affirmative, now in the negative, now with a simultaneous yes and no. There are no general rules; there are only particular cases; and most of these cases exist, so far as we are concerned, in a thick night of ignorance.

Here, for example, is the case that presents itself to every tourist who goes to Rome—the fascinatingly enigmatic case of baroque art and seventeenth-century Catholicism. In what way were the two related? What was the nature of the connection between the art forms of the period and the religious experiences of those who lived through it?

Three hundred years after the event all that we know for certain is that the personages represented in baroque religious art are all in a state of chronic emotional excitement. They wave their arms, roll their eyes, press hands to palpitating bosoms, sometimes, in an excess of feeling, swoon away into unconsciousness. We look at them with a mixture of aesthetic admiration and moral distaste, then start to speculate about the men and women who were contemporary with them. Was their religious life as wildly agitated as the life of these creatures of the painters' and sculptors' imagination? And, if so, had the art been modelled on their agitation, or was their agitation due to familiarity with an art that had become agitated for purely aesthetic reasons? Or, finally, was there no agitation in the real world corresponding to that prevailing in the worlds of painting and sculpture? Baroque artists were tired of doing what their predecessors had done and were committed by the inner logic of their tradition to an exploration of the inordinate; therefore the figures above the altars had to gesticulate in a studied frenzy. But the religious life of the people who worshipped at those altars—had that become significantly different from the religious life of the men and women of other periods? Were there not then, as always, a few ardent contemplatives and actives, imperfectly leavening a great lump of the legalistic and the corybantic, the time-serving and the lukewarm?

I myself incline to the last alternative. Environment is never the sole determinant, and heredity is always at work, producing every variety of physique and temperament at every period of history. All the potentialities of human nature exist at all times, and at all times (in spite of an environment which may be unfavourable to some of them) practically all the potentialities are to some extent actualized. One has only to read Salimbene's *Chronicle* and Law's *Serious Call* in order to realize that there were as many irreligious people in the ages of faith as there were pietists in the ages of reason. The Byzantines who went mad about trinitarian theology were the same Byzantines who went mad about the chariot races. And our own age of atomic physics is also a notable age of astrology and numerology. At every period there exists, not a synthesis, but a mere brute collocation of opposites and incompatibles. And yet at any given epoch there is only one prevailing style of art, in terms of which painters and sculptors treat of a strictly limited number of subjects. Art may be defined, in this context, as a process of selection and transformation, whereby an unmanageable multiplicity is reduced to a semblance, at least, of unity. Consequently we must never expect to find in art a reflection of contemporary reality as it is actually experienced by human beings in all their congenital and acquired variety. Thus, from a study of the restrained and formalized art of the Italian *trecento*, who could infer the existence of those wild religious revivals which were so characteristic a feature of the period? And, conversely, who from the frenzies of the baroque could infer the facts of sixteenth- and seventeenth-century mysticism? Looking at a Carlo Dolci Magdalen, who could guess what St. John of the Cross had said about true Charity—that it is a matter, not of feeling, but of the will? Or who, with Bernini's St. Teresa before his eyes, would ever suspect that Bernini's contemporary, Charles de Condren, had deplored the weakness which caused ecstatics to receive God *si animalement*? The truth would seem to be that while the great masses of the people remained, as ever, indifferent or fitfully superstitious, and while the masters of the spiritual life preached a worship of the Spirit in spirit, the artists of the time chose to glorify a Christianity of thrills and visceral yearnings, now violent, now cloyingly sentimental. And they chose to do so for reasons connected, not with the problems of life, but with those of art. Their painting and sculpture did not, and indeed could not, reflect the manifold religious experience of the time, nor did the religious experience of most of their contemporaries reflect the prevailing art. Art and religious life went their separate ways, the artists using religion as their opportunity for developing a baroque expressionism, and the religious using this art as an instrument for achieving the various kinds of experience for which their temperaments had fitted them. And precisely the same relations between religion and art had existed when the 'Primitives' were using a multiform Catholicism as an opportunity for creating one particular kind of static composition, and when the religious were using these works as instruments for the practice now of revivalism, now of contemplation, now of magic.

From Rome and the baroque let us pass for a moment to Tuscany and the rococo. A few miles from Siena there stands among the vineyards a large Carthusian monastery, called Pontignano, now inhabited by a score of peasant families. In the old days each of the monks occupied an apartment of three rooms—a kitchen, a bedroom and a tiny oratory. The front doors of these apartments give on to the cloisters, and at the back are little walled gardens, where a man could grow vegetables and dig his own grave. Every brother lived independently of all the rest, a solitary in a community of solitaries, a mute among the silent. Most of the buildings at Pontignano date from the fourteenth century, but were re-furbished by an interior decorator of the eighteenth. Under his direction the church was adorned with an enormous high altar of wood, painted to look like marble, and the little oratories, in which the monks said their private prayers, were stuccoed over with rococo twiddles, till they looked like the boudoirs of so many provincial Pompadours. To us, with our incorrigible sense of history, this conjunction of St. Bruno and Louis XV seems deliriously incongruous. But how did it strike the monks who actually prayed in those oratories? Did they suddenly start to think, feel and behave like those libertine *abbés* whom we associate with that kind of decoration? Surely not. "Never reformed, because never deformed," the Carthusian order held on its way regardless of changes in aesthetic fashion. In their newly plastered oratories the brethren meditated on death, just as their predecessors had meditated when the decorations were Baroque or Renaissance, Gothic or Romanesque. Styles change, empires rise and fall; but death remains itself, a brute fact, sooner or later, of every individual's experience—a fact that has no history and to which, in consequence, all historical changes, whether political or economic, scientific or artistic, are completely irrelevant. The Pompadourish art in the Pontignano oratories tells us nothing whatever about contemporary Carthusian religion, which was centred, as ever, upon the contemplation of death. All we learn from it is that, when eighteenth-century monks found it necessary to restore ancient buildings, the only restorers available, in an age that was still innocent of pastiche and antiquarian forgery, were men brought up in the current tradition of art.

In our own days the religious are worse off than were

the monks of Pontignano. Not living Rococo, but the bogus-mediaeval, or some atrocious piece of mass-produced *bondieuserie*, is all that they can find for their purposes. And yet, in spite of the nullity of modern religious art, religion, in all its aspects from the fetishistic to the contemplative, continues to flourish and to produce its good or evil fruits. Man is a whole, and so, perhaps, is society; but they are wholes divided, like ships, into water-tight compartments. On one side of a bulkhead is art, on the other religion. There may be good wine in one compartment, bilge-water in the other. The connection between the two is not by pipe or osmosis, but only from above, only for the intellect that looks down and can see both simultaneously and recognize them as belonging (by juxtaposition rather than by fusion) to the same individual or social whole.

VARIATIONS ON A BAROQUE TOMB

"THE skeleton," as we all know, "was invisible in the happy days of pagan art." And invisible it remained, in spite of Christianity, for most of the centuries that followed. Throughout the Middle Ages, the knights, the mitred bishops, the ladies who warm their feet on the backs of little dogs—all are reassuringly in the flesh. No skulls adorn their tombs, no bones, no grisly reapers. Artists in words may cry, "Alas, my heart will break in three: *Terribilis Mors conturbat me.*" Artists in stone are content to carve the likeness of a sleeper upon a bed. The Renaissance comes and still the sleep persists, tranquil amid the sculptured dreams of a paradise half earthly, half celestial.

> *Those Pans and Nymphs ye wot of, and perchance*
> *Some tripod, thyrsus, with a vase or so,*
> *The Saviour at his sermon on the mount,*
> *St. Praxed in a glory, and one Pan*
> *Ready to twitch the Nymph's last garment off,*
> *And Moses with the tables.*

But by the middle of the sixteenth century a change has taken place. The effigy no longer sleeps, but opens its eyes and sits up—ideally noble, as on the Medicean tombs, or soberly a portrait, like any one of those admirable busts in their round niches between the pilasters of a classical design. And, at the base, below the Latin inscription, it not infrequently happens (at any rate in

Rome and after 1550) that a little skull, in bone-white marble, reminds the onlooker of what he himself will soon be, of what the original of the portrait has already become.

Why should the death's-head have become fashionable at this particular moment of history? The religiously minded might surmise that it had something to do with the Counter-Reformation; the medically minded, that it was connected with that sixteenth-century pandemic of syphilis, whose noseless victims were a constant reminder of man's latter end; the artistically minded, that some mortuary sculptor of the time had a taste for, and a happy knack with, bones. I do not venture to decide between the possible alternatives, but am content to record the fact, observable by anyone who has been in Rome, that there, after the middle of the century, the skulls indubitably are.

As the years pass these reminders of mortality assume an ever greater importance. From being miniatures they grow in a short time into full-blown, death-sized replicas of the thing behind the face. And suddenly, imitating those bodiless seraphs of mediaeval and renaissance painting, they sprout a pair of wings and learn to fly. And meanwhile the art of the late Renaissance has become the Baroque. By an aesthetic necessity, because it is impossible for self-conscious artists to go on doing what has been supremely well done by their predecessors, the symmetrical gives place to the disbalanced, the static to the dynamic, the formalized to the realistic. Statues are caught in the act of changing their positions; pictorial compositions try to break out of their frames. Where there was understatement, there is now emphasis; where there was measure and humanity, there is now the enormous, the astounding, the demi-god and the epileptic sub-man.

Consider, for example, those skulls on the monuments. They have grown in size; their truth to death is overpowering and, to heighten the effect of verisimilitude, the sculptor has shifted them from their old place on the central axis and now shows them, casual and unposed, in profile or three-quarters face, looking up to heaven or down into the grave. And their wings! Vast, wildly beating, wind-blown—the wings of vultures in a hurricane. The appetite for the inordinate grows with what it feeds upon, and along with it grow the virtuosity of the artists and the willingness of their patrons to pay for ever more astounding monuments. By 1630 the skull is no longer adequate as a *memento mori*; it has become necessary to represent the entire skeleton.

The most grandiose of these reminders of our mortality are the mighty skeletons which Bernini made for the tombs of Urban VIII and Alexander VII in St. Peter's. Majestic in his vestments and intensely alive, each of the two Popes sits there aloft, blessing his people. Some feet below him, on either side, are his special Virtues—Faith, Temperance, Fortitude, who knows? In the middle, below the Pontiff, is the gigantic emblem of death. On Urban's tomb the skeleton is holding (slightly cock-eyed, for it would be intolerably old-fashioned and unrealistic if the thing were perfectly level) a black marble scroll inscribed with the Pope's name and title; on Alexander's the monster has been 'stopped,' as the photographers say, in the act of shooting up from the doorway leading into the vault. Up it comes, like a rocket, at an angle of sixty or seventy degrees, and as it rises it effortlessly lifts six or seven tons of the red marble drapery, which mitigates the rigidities of architecture and transforms the statically geometrical into something mobile and indeterminate.

The emphasis, in these two extraordinary works, is not on heaven, hell and purgatory, but on physical dissolution and the grave. The terror which inspired such works as the *Dies Irae* was of the second death, the death inflicted by an angry judge upon the sinner's soul. Here, on the contrary, the theme is the first death, the abrupt passage from animation to insensibility and from worldly glory to supper with the convocation of politic worms.

Chi un tempo, carco d'amorose prede,
ebbe l'ostro alle guance e l'oro al crine,
deforme, arido teschio, ecco, si vede.

Bernini's tombs are by no means unique. The Roman churches are full of cautionary skeletons. In Santa Maria sopra Minerva, for example, there is a small monument attached to one of the columns on the north side of the church. It commemorates a certain Vizzani, if I remember rightly, a jurisconsult who died some time before the middle of the seventeenth century. Here, as in the wall monuments of the High Renaissance, a bust looks out of a rounded niche placed above the long Latin catalogue of the dead man's claims upon the attention of posterity. It is the bust, so intensely lifelike as to be almost a caricature, of a florid individual in his middle forties, no fool evidently, but wearing an expression of serene and unquestioning complacency. Socially, professionally, financially, what a huge success his life has been! And how strongly, like Milton, he feels that "nothing profits more than self-esteem founded on just and right." But suddenly we become aware that the bust in its round frame is being held in an almost amorous embrace by a great skeleton in high relief, whizzing diagonally, from left to right, across the monument. The lawyer and all his achievements, all his self-satisfaction, are being wafted away into darkness and oblivion.

Of the same kind, but still more astounding, are the tombs of the Pallavicini family in San Francesco a Ripa. Executed by Mazzuoli at the beginning of the eighteenth century, these monuments are among the last and at the same time the most extravagant outflowerings of the baroque spirit. Admirably carved, the usual Virtues keep guard at the base of each of the vast pyramidal structures. Above them, flapping huge wings, a ten-foot skeleton in bronze holds up for our inspection a pair of oval frames, containing busts of the departed Pallavicini. On one side of the family chapel we see the likenesses of two princely ecclesiastics. Death holds them with a studied carelessness, tilting their frames a little, one to the left, the other to the right, so that the grave ascetic faces look out, as though through the ports of a rolling ship. Opposite them, in the hands of another and, if possible, even more frightful skeleton, are two more members of the family—an elderly princess, this time, and her spouse. And what a spouse! Under the majestic wig the face is gross, many-chinned, complacently imbecile. High blood-pressure inflates the whole squat person almost to bursting point; pride keeps the pig-snout chronically pointing to the skies. And it is Death who now holds him aloft; it is Corruption who, with triumphant derision, exhibits him, for ever pilloried in marble, a grotesque and pitiable example of human bumptiousness.

Looking at the little fat man up there in the skeleton's clutches, one reflects, with a certain astonishment, that some Pallavicino must have ordered and presumably paid for this strange monument to a departed relative. With what intentions? To display the absurdity of the old gentleman's pretensions to grandeur? To make a mock of everything he had lived for? The answer to these questions is, at least in part, affirmative. All these baroque tombs were doctrinally sound. The heirs of popes and princes laid out huge sums to celebrate the glories of their distinguished forebears—but laid them out on monuments whose emphatically Christian theme is the transience of earthly greatness and the vanity of human wishes. After which they addressed themselves with redoubled energy to the task of satisfying their own cravings for money, position and power. A belief in hell and the knowledge that every ambition is doomed to frustration at the hands of a skeleton have never prevented the majority of human beings from behaving as though death were no more than an unfounded rumour and survival a thing beyond the bounds of possibility. The men of the Baroque differed from those of other epochs not in what they actually did, not even in what they thought about those doings, but in what they were ready to express of their thoughts. They liked an art that harps on death and corruption and were neither better nor worse than we who are reticent about such things.

The fantastic dance of death in San Francesco a Ripa is almost the last of its kind. Thirty years after it was carved, Robert Blair could achieve a modest popularity by writing such lines as these:

> *Methinks I see thee with thy head low laid,*
> *While surfeited upon thy damask cheek*
> *The high-fed worm, in lazy volumes rolled,*
> *Riots unscared.*

But eighteenth-century sculptors made no attempt to realize these gruesome images. On graves and monuments Death no longer comments upon the mad pretensions of his victims. Broken columns, extinguished torches, weeping angels and muses—these are now the emblems in vogue. The artist and his patron are concerned to evoke sentiments less painful than the horror of corruption. With the nineteenth century we enter an age of stylistic revivals; but there is never a return to the mortuary fashions of the Baroque. From the time of Mazzuoli until the present day no monument to any important European has been adorned with death's heads or skeletons.

We live habitually on at least three levels—the level of strictly individual existence, the level of intellectual abstraction and the level of historical necessity and social convention. On the first of these levels our life is completely private; on the others it is, at least partially, a shared and public life. Thus, writing about death, I am on the level of intellectual abstraction. Participating in the life of a generation, to which the mortuary art of the Baroque seems odd and alien, I am on the level of history. But when I actually come to die, I shall be on the first level, the level of exclusively individual experience. That which, in human life, is shared and public has always been regarded as more respectable than that which is private. Kings have their Astronomers Royal, Emperors their official Historiographers; but there are no Royal Gastronomers, no Papal or Imperial Pornographers. Among crimes, the social and the historical are condoned as last infirmities of noble mind, and their perpetrators are very generally admired. The lustful and intemperate, on the contrary, are condemned by all—even by themselves (which was why Jesus so much preferred them to the respectable Pharisees). We have no God of Brothels, but the God of Battles, alas, is still going strong.

Baroque mortuary sculpture has as its basic subject-matter the conflict, on one important front, between the public and the private, between the social and the individual, between the historical and the existential. The prince in his curly wig, the Pope in his vestments, the lawyer with his Latin eulogy and his smirk of self-satisfaction—all these are pillars of society, representatives of great historical forces and even makers of history. But under smirk and wig and tiara is the body with its unshareable physiological processes, is the psyche with its insights and sudden graces, its abysmal imbecilities and its unavowable desires. Every public figure—and to some extent we are all public figures—is also an island universe of private experiences; and the most private of all these experiences is that of falling out of history, of being separated from society—in a word, the experience of death.

Based as they always are upon ignorance—invincible in some cases, voluntary and selective in others—historical generalizations can never be more than partially true. In spite of which and at the risk of distorting the facts to fit a theory, I would suggest that, at any given period, preoccupation with death is in inverse ratio to the prevalence of a belief in man's perfectibility through and in a properly organized society. In the art and literature of the age of Condorcet, of the age of Herbert Spencer and Karl Marx, of the age of Lenin and the Webbs there are few skeletons. Why? Because it was during the eighteenth and nineteenth centuries that men came to believe in progress, in the march of history towards an ever bigger and better future, in salvation, not for the individual, but for society. The emphasis is on history and environment, which are regarded as the primary determinants of individual destiny. Indeed, among orthodox Marxians they are now (since the canonization of Lysenko and the anathema pronounced on 'reactionary Morganism') regarded as the sole determinants. Predestination, whether Augustinian or Mendelian, whether *karmic* or genetic, has been ruled out, and we are back with Helvétius and his shepherd boys who can all be transformed into Newtons, back with Dr. Watson and his infinitely conditionable infants. But meanwhile the fact remains that, in this still unregenerate world, each of us inherits a physique and a temperament. Moreover, the career of every individual man or woman is essentially non-progressive. We reach maturity only to decline into decrepitude and the body's death. Could anything be more painfully obvious? And yet how rarely in the course of the last two hundred and fifty years has death been made the theme of any considerable work of art! Among the great painters only Goya has chosen to treat of death, and then only of death by violence, death in war. The mortuary sculptors, as we have seen, harp only

M

on the sentiments surrounding death—sentiments ranging from the noble to the tender and even the voluptuous. (The most delicious buttocks in the whole repertory of art are to be found on Canova's monument to the last of the Stuarts.)

In the literature of this same period death has been handled more frequently than in painting or sculpture, but only once (to my knowledge, at least) with complete adequacy. Tolstoy's *The Death of Ivan Ilyitch* is one of the artistically most perfect and at the same time one of the most terrible books ever written. It is the story of an utterly commonplace man who is compelled to discover, step by agonizing step, that the public personage with whom, all his life, he has identified himself is hardly more than a figment of the collective imagination, and that his essential self is the solitary, insulated being who falls sick and suffers, rejects and is rejected by the world and finally (for the story has a happy ending) gives in to his destiny, and in the act of surrender, at the very moment of death, finds himself alone and naked in the presence of the Light. The baroque sculptors are concerned with the same theme; but they protest too much and their conscious striving for sublimity is apt to defeat its own object. Tolstoy is never emphatic, indulges in no rhetorical flourishes, speaks simply of the most difficult matters and flatly, matter-of-factly, of the most terrible. That is why his book has such power and is so profoundly disturbing to our habitual complacency. We are shocked by it in much the same way as we are shocked by pornography—and for the same reason. Sex is almost as completely private a matter as death, and a work of art which powerfully expresses the truth about either of them is very painful to the respectable public figure we imagine ourselves to be. Nobody can have the consolations of religion or philosophy unless he has first experienced their desolations. And nothing is more desolating than a thorough knowledge of the private self. Hence the utility of such books as *Ivan Ilyitch* and, I would venture to add, such books as Henry Miller's *Tropic of Cancer*.

And here let me add a parenthetical note on the pornography of the age which witnessed the rise of the ideas of progress and social salvation. Most of it is merely pretty, an affair of wish-fulfilments—Boucher carried to his logical conclusion. The most celebrated pornographer of the time, the Marquis de Sade, is a mixture of escapist maniac and *philosophe*. He lives in a world where insane phantasy alternates with post-Voltairean ratiocination; where impossible orgies are interrupted in order that the participants may talk, sometimes shrewdly, but more often in the shallowest eighteenth-century way, about morals, politics and metaphysics. Here, for example, is a typical specimen of Sadian sociology. "Is incest dangerous? Certainly not. It extends family ties and consequently renders more active the citizen's love of his fatherland." In this passage, as throughout the work of this oddest product of the Enlightenment, we see the public figure doing his silly best to rationalize the essentially unrationalizable facts of private existence. But what we need, if we are to know ourselves, is the truthful and penetrating expression in art of precisely these unrationalizable facts—the facts of death, as in *Ivan Ilyitch*, the facts of sex, as in *Tropic of Cancer*, the facts of pain and cruelty, as in Goya's *Disasters*, the facts of fear and disgust and fatigue, as in that most horrifyingly truthful of war-books, *The Naked and the Dead.* Ignorance is a bliss we can never afford; but to know only ourselves is not enough. If it is to be a fruitful desolation, self-knowledge must be made the road to a knowledge of the Other. Unmitigated, it is but another form of ignorance and can lead only to despair or complacent cynicism. Floundering between time and eternity, we are amphibians and must accept the fact. *Noverim me, noverim Te*—the prayer expresses an essentially realistic attitude towards the universe in which, willy-nilly, we have to live and to die.

Death is not the only private experience with which baroque art concerns itself. A few yards from the Pallavicino tombs reclines Bernini's statue of Blessed Ludovica Albertoni in ecstasy. Here, as in the case of the same artist's more celebrated St. Teresa, the experience recorded is of a privacy so special that, at a first glance, the spectator feels a shock of embarrassment. Entering those rich chapels in San Francesco and Santa Maria della Vittoria, one has the impression of having opened a bedroom door at the most inopportune of moments, almost of having opened *Tropic of Cancer* at one of its most startling pages. The posture of the ecstatics, their expression and the exuberance of the tripe-like drapery which surrounds them and, in the Albertoni's case, overflows in a kind of peritoneal cataract on to the altar below—all conspire to emphasize the fact that, though saints may be important historical figures, their physiology is as disquietingly private as anyone else's.

By the inner logic of the tradition within which they worked, baroque artists were committed to a systematic exploitation of the inordinate. Hence the epileptic be-

This experience is, of course, perfectly private, non-historical and unsocial. That is why, to the organizers of Churches and the exponents of salvation through the State, it has always seemed so suspect, shady and even indecent. And yet, like sex and pain and death, there it remains, one of the brute facts with which, whether we like them or not, we have to come to terms. Maddeningly, unbearably, an occasional artist rubs our noses in his rendering of these facts. Confronted by the pornographies of suffering, of sensuality, of dissolution, by *The Disasters of War* and *The Naked and the Dead*, by *Tropic of Cancer*, by *Ivan Ilyitch* and even (despite their ludicrous sublimity) by the baroque tombs, we shrink and are appalled. And in another way there is something hardly less appalling in the pornographies (as many good rationalists regard them) of mysticism. Even the consolations of religion and philosophy are pretty desolating for the average sensual man, who clings to his ignorance as the sole guarantee of happiness. *Terribilis Mors conturbat me*; but so does *terribilis Vita*.

VARIATIONS ON EL GRECO

IN 1541, when Domenikos Theotokopoulos was born, his native island of Crete had been for more than three centuries under Venetian rule. Trade had followed the imperial flag, but not culture. In language, in thought, in art, the island remained as what it had been ever since the People of the Sea finally broke the Minoan power—a part of Greece. In the Cretan schools young men studied the philosophers of ancient Athens and the theologians of Christian Byzantium, Byzantine paintings and Byzantine mosaics adorned the churches, and even in the revolutionary sixteenth century the Cretan artists went their traditional way without paying the smallest attention to what had been happening in near-by Italy. Their pictures were two-dimensional, non-realistic, innocent of perspective and chiaroscuro. So far as they were concerned, Giotto and Masaccio, to say nothing of Raphael and Michelangelo and Titian, might never have existed.

Young Domenikos received a sound Greek education and studied painting under the best masters of the island. Not, however, for very long. In Candia one could see, along with the other importations from the mainland, examples of Venetian painting. The orthodox might shake their heads. What a way to treat the Mother of God! And that indecently human personage—was that supposed to be the Pantocrator? But to a young man of original and enquiring mind their very unorthodoxy must have seemed attractive. They were tokens from a world where the artist was his own master, where too he might make technical experiments, where he was free to see and represent all the things which, for the Byzantines, simply didn't exist. Moreover, this world of artistic liberty was also a world where a man could make his fortune. Venice was rich; Crete, miserably poor. There was no future for a man in Candia; but on the mainland, on the mainland . . .

In the early fifteen-sixties, when the young immigrant from Crete first stepped ashore, Venice was at the height of her artistic glory. Titian was a very old man, but painting as well as, or indeed better than, he had ever done in his youth. Tintoretto, his junior by forty years, was hard at work, transforming the principles of High Renaissance composition into those of the Baroque. Still in his youthful prime, Veronese was effortlessly turning out enormous masterpieces of decorative art. "Bliss was it in that dawn to be alive." But, all dawns—the artistic no less than the political, the religious, the sexual—give place to mornings, afternoons and nights. After having worked for several years as "a disciple of Titian" (to use the phrase by which he was later to be described) Domenikos came to be profoundly dissatisfied with Venetian art. It could hardly have been otherwise. By nature introspective, by nurture a Christian Neo-Platonist and a student of Byzantine art, the young man might admire Venetian technique, but could never approve the uses to which that technique was put. For his taste Venetian art was too pagan, too voluptuous, too decorative, too much concerned with appearances, insufficiently inward and serious. In search of an art more conformable to his own nature and ideals Domenikos migrated in

1570 to Rome. But Rome, alas, proved to be no less disappointing than Venice. The great masters of the High Renaissance were all dead, and their successors were second-rate mannerists, incapable of creating anything new and living parasitically upon the achievements of the past. For Domenikos, the living were without interest and even the mighty dead were not the masters he had been looking for. Of Michelangelo, for example, he complained that the man did not know how to paint—which is a rather violent way of expressing the unquestionable truth that Michelangelo was primarily a sculptor and that his paintings are in some sort translations of sculpture into a language which was not the artist's native tongue. To a young man whose vocation was to express himself, not in marble, not in transcriptions of sculpture, but in colour and the rich texture of oil pigments, the frescoes of the Sistine Chapel were not very instructive.

The artist's stay in Rome lasted for several years. Then, at some date prior to 1577, he undertook yet another migration, this time to Spain. Why to Spain? As usual, we do not know. And when, some years later, during a lawsuit, the same question was put to El Greco himself, he declined to answer. Evidently he was of the opinion that people should mind their own business.

The Cretan's wanderings were now at an end. He settled in Toledo, and there with his wife, Jeronima de las Cuevas, and his son, Jorge Manuel, he remained until his death in 1614. Of his life in Spain we know only a very little more than we know of his life in Crete and Italy—that is to say, next to nothing. Here are some of the scanty odds and ends of information that have come down to us.

Professionally, El Greco was successful. Many commissions came his way and he was well paid for his work. On several occasions he went to law with his ecclesiastical patrons in order to get his price. He had the reputation of spending his money with a lordly extravagance, and it was said that he paid an orchestra to make music while he ate his meals. His apartment on the verge of the great canyon of the Tagus contained twenty-four rooms, most of which, however, were left almost completely unfurnished. Of his own genius he had no doubts. He knew that he painted superlatively well and he was quite ready to say so in public. Moreover, when Philip II and certain of the clergy objected to his pictures on the ground that they did not respect the norms of ecclesiastical art, he steadfastly refused to compromise and went on painting exactly as he thought fit. Like Tintoretto, he modelled small clay figures, with the aid of which he studied effects of lighting and foreshortening. Pacheco, the father-in-law of Velasquez, saw a whole cupboardful of these figures when he visited El Greco shortly before the latter's death. Needless to say, they have all disappeared and along with them has gone the treatise which El Greco wrote on painting. Among the painter's friends were poets, men of learning, eminent ecclesiastics. His library, as we know from the inventory which was made after his death, contained, among other Greek works, the famous *Mystical Theology* of Dionysius the Areopagite, together with more recent Italian books on Neo-Platonic philosophy. In the light of this fact, a curious anecdote recorded by Giulio Clovio, one of El Greco's Roman friends, takes on a special significance. "Yesterday," wrote Clovio in a letter which is still extant, "I called at his (El Greco's) lodgings to take him for a walk through the city. The weather was very fine. . . . But on entering the studio I was amazed to find the curtains so closely drawn that it was hardly possible to see anything. The painter was sitting in a chair, neither working nor sleeping, and declined to go out with me on the ground that the light of day disturbed his inward light." From this it would appear that El Greco took more than a theoretical interest in the mystical states described by Dionysius and the Neo-Platonists; he also practised some form of meditation.

Of El Greco's personal appearance we know nothing for certain. The so-called 'self-portrait' may perhaps represent the painter's features; or, on the other hand, it may not. The evidence is inconclusive. At every turn the man eludes us. Only his work remains.

A representational picture is one that 'tells a story'—the story, for example, of the Nativity, the story of Mars and Venus, the story of a certain landscape or a certain person as they appeared at a certain moment of time. But this story is never the whole story. A picture always expresses more than is implicit in its subject. Every painter who tells a story tells it in his own manner, and that manner tells another story superimposed, as it were, upon the first—a story about the painter himself, a story about the way in which one highly gifted individual reacted to his experience of our universe. The first story is told deliberately; the second tells itself independently of the artist's conscious will. He cannot help telling it; for it is the expression of his own intimate being—of the temperament with which he was born, the character which he himself has forged and the unconscious tendencies formed by the interaction of temperament, character and outward circumstances.

Like most of his predecessors and contemporaries, El Greco was mainly a religious painter, a teller of old familiar stories, from the Gospels and the legends of the saints. But he told it in his own peculiar manner, and that manner tells another story, so enigmatic that we pore over it in fascinated bewilderment, trying to construe its meaning.

In looking at any of the great compositions of El Greco's maturity, we must always remember that the intention of the artist was neither to imitate nature nor to tell a story with dramatic verisimilitude. Like the Post-Impressionists three centuries later, El Greco used natural objects as the raw material out of which, by a process of calculated distortion, he might create his own world of pictorial forms in pictorial space under pictorial illumination. Within this private universe he situated his religious subject-matter, using it as a vehicle for expressing what he wanted to say about life.

And what *did* El Greco want to say? The answer can only be inferred; but to me, at least, it seems sufficiently clear. Those faces with their uniformly rapturous expression, those hands clasped in devotion or lifted towards heaven, those figures stretched out to the point where the whole inordinately elongated anatomy becomes a living symbol of upward aspiration—all these bear witness to the artist's constant preoccupation with the ideas of mystical religion. His aim is to assert the soul's capacity to come, through effort and through grace, to ecstatic union with the divine Spirit. This idea of union is more and more emphatically stressed as the painter advances in years. The frontier between earth and heaven, which is clearly defined in such works as *The Burial of Count Orgaz* and *The Dream of Philip II*, grows fainter and finally disappears. In the latest version of Christ's Baptism there is no separation of any kind. The forms and colours flow continuously from the bottom of the picture to the top. The two realms are totally fused.

Does this mean that El Greco actually found a perfect pictorial expression for what his contemporary, St. Teresa of Avila, called 'the spiritual marriage'? I think not. For all their extraordinary beauty, these great paintings are strangely oppressive and disquieting. Consciously El Greco was telling two stories—a story from the Gospels or the legends of the saints, and a story about mystical union with the divine. But, unconsciously, he told yet another story, having little or nothing to do with the two he knew he was telling. All that is disquieting in El Greco pertains to this third story and is conveyed to the spectator by his highly individual manner of treating space and the forms by which that space is occupied.

In the Byzantine art, with which El Greco was familiar in his youth, there is no third dimension. The figures in the icons and mosaics are the inhabitants of a Flatland in which there is no question of perspective. And precisely because there is no perspective, these figures seem to exist in a celestial universe having implications of indefinite extension. From ancient and conservative Byzantium El Greco travelled through time as well as space to modern Venice. Here, in Titian's paintings, he found the realistic representation of a third dimension travelling back from the picture-plane to far-away landscapes of blue mountains under majestic clouds. And in Tintoretto's compositions he could study those rocketing centrifugal movements that carry the spectator's mind beyond the picture-frame and suggest the endless succession of things and spaces existing in the world outside.

The nature of El Greco's personality was such that he chose to combine Byzantium and Venice in the strangest possible way. His pictures are neither flat nor fully three-dimensional. There is depth in his private universe, but only a very little of it. From the picture-plane to the remotest object in the background there is, in most cases, an apparent distance of only a few feet. On earth, as in heaven, there is hardly room to swing a cat. Moreover, unlike Tintoretto and the baroque artists of the seventeenth century, El Greco never hints at the boundlessness beyond the picture-frame. His compositions are centripetal, turned inwards on themselves. He is the painter of movement in a narrow room, of agitation in prison. This effect of confinement is enhanced by the almost complete absence from his paintings of a landscape background. The whole picture-space is tightly packed with figures, human and divine; and where any chink is left between body and body, we are shown only a confining wall of cloud as opaque as earth, or of earth as fluidly plastic as the clouds. So far as El Greco is concerned, the world of non-human nature is practically non-existent.

No less disquieting than the narrowness of El Greco's universe is the quality of the forms with which he filled it. Everything here is organic, but organic on a low level, organic to a point well below the limit of life's perfection. That is why there is no sensuality in these paintings, nothing of the voluptuous. In a work of art we are charmed and attracted by forms which represent or at least suggest the forms of such objects as we find attractive in nature—flowers, for example, fruits, animals, human bodies in their youthful strength and beauty. In life we are not at all attracted by protoplasm in the raw or by individual organs separated from the organism as a whole. But it is with forms suggestive precisely of such objects that El Greco fills his pictures. Under his brush the human body, when it is naked, loses its bony framework and even its musculature, and becomes a thing of ectoplasm—beautifully appropriate in its strange pictorial context, but not a little uncanny when thought of in the context of real life. And when El Greco clothes his boneless creatures, their draperies become pure abstractions, having the form of something indeterminately physiological.

And here a brief parenthesis is in order. A painter or a sculptor can be simultaneously representational and nonrepresentational. In their architectural backgrounds and, above all, in their draperies, many works, even of the Renaissance and the Baroque, incorporate passages of almost unadulterated abstraction. These are often expressive in the highest degree. Indeed, the whole tone of a representational work may be established, and its inner meaning expressed, by those parts of it which are most nearly abstract. Thus, the pictures of Piero della Francesca leave upon us an impression of calm, of power, of intellectual objectivity and stoical detachment. From

The Baptism of Christ
By El Greco

those of Cosimo Tura there emanates a sense of disquiet, even of anguish. When we analyse the purely pictorial reasons for our perception of a profound difference in the temperaments of the two artists, we find that a very important part is played by the least representational elements in their pictures—the draperies. In Piero's draperies there are large unbroken surfaces, and the folds are designed to emphasize the elementary solid-geometrical structure of the figures. In Tura's draperies the surfaces are broken up, and there is a profusion of sharp angles, of jagged and flame-like forms. Something analogous may be found in the work of two great painters of a later period, Poussin and Watteau. Watteau's draperies are broken into innumerable tiny folds and wrinkles, so that the colour of a mantle or a doublet is never the same for half an inch together. The impression left upon the spectator is one of extreme sensibility and the most delicate refinement. Poussin's much broader treatment of these almost non-representational accessories seems to express a more masculine temperament and a philosophy of life akin to Piero's noble stoicism.

In some works the non-representational passages are actually more important than the representational. Thus in many of Bernini's statues, only the hands, feet and face are fully representational; all the rest is drapery—that is to say, a writhing and undulant abstraction. It is the same with El Greco's paintings. In some of them a third, a half, even as much as two-thirds of the entire surface is occupied by low-level organic abstractions, to which, because of their representational context, we give the name of draperies, or clouds, or rocks. These abstractions are powerfully expressive and it is through them that, to a considerable extent, El Greco tells the private story that underlies the official subject-matter of his paintings.

At this point the pure abstractionist will come forward with a question. Seeing that the non-representational passages in representational works are so expressive, why should anyone bother with representation? Why trouble to tell a high-level story about recognizable objects when the more important low-level story about the artist's temperament and reactions to life can be told in terms of pure abstractions? I myself have no objection to pure abstractions which, in the hands of a gifted artist, can achieve their own kind of aesthetic perfection. But this perfection, it seems to me, is a perfection within rather narrow limits. The Greeks called the circle 'a perfect figure.' And so it is—one cannot improve on it. And yet a composition consisting of a red circle inscribed within a black square would strike us, for all its perfection, as being a little dull. Even aesthetically the perfect figure of a circle is less interesting than the perfect figure of a young woman. This does not mean, of course, that the representation of the young woman by a bad artist will be more valuable, as a picture, than a composition of circles, squares and triangles devised by a good one. But it does mean, I think, that nature is a richer source of forms than any text-book of plane or solid geometry. Nature has evolved innumerable forms and, as we ourselves move from point to point, we see large numbers of these forms, grouped in an endless variety of ways and thus creating an endless variety of new forms, all of which may be used as the raw materials of works of art. What is given is incomparably richer than what we can invent. But the richness of nature is, from our point of view, a chaos upon which we, as philosophers, men of science, technicians and artists, must impose various kinds of unity. Now, I would say that, other things being equal, a work of art which imposes aesthetic unity upon a large number of formal and psychological elements is a greater and more interesting work than one in which unity is imposed upon only a few elements. In other words, there is a hierarchy of perfections. Bach's Two-Part Inventions are perfect in their way. But his Chromatic Fantasia is also perfect; and since its perfection involves the imposition of aesthetic unity upon a larger number of elements it is (as we all in fact recognize) a greater work. The old distinction between the Fine Arts and the crafts is based to some extent upon snobbery and other non-aesthetic considerations. But not entirely. In the hierarchy of perfections a perfect vase or a perfect carpet occupies a lower rank than that, say, of Giotto's frescoes at Padua, or Rembrandt's *Polish Rider*, or the *Grande Jatte* of Georges Seurat. In these and a hundred other masterpieces of painting the pictorial whole embraces and unifies a repertory of forms much more numerous, varied, strange and interesting than those which come together in the wholes organized by even the most gifted craftsmen. And, over and above this richer and subtler formal perfection, we are presented with a non-pictorial bonus of a story and, explicit or implicit, a criticism of life. At their best, non-representational compositions achieve perfection; but it is a perfection nearer to that of the jug or rug than to that of the enormously complex and yet completely unified masterpieces of representational art—most of which, as we have seen, contain expressive passages of almost pure abstraction. At the present time it would seem that the most sensible and rewarding thing for a painter to do is (like Braque, for example) to make the best and the most of both worlds, representational as well as non-representational.

Within his own Byzantine-Venetian tradition El Greco did precisely this, combining representation with abstraction in a manner which we are accustomed to regard as characteristically modern. His intention, as we have seen, was to use this powerful artistic instrument to express, in visual terms, man's capacity for union with the divine. But the artistic means he employed were such that it was not possible for him to carry out that intention. The existence of a spiritual reality transcendent and yet immanent, absolutely other and yet the sustaining spiritual essence of every being, has frequently been rendered in visual symbols—but not symbols of the kind employed by El Greco. The agitation of quasi-visceral forms in an overcrowded and almost spaceless world from which non-human nature has been banished cannot, in the very nature of things, express man's union with the Spirit who must be worshipped in spirit.

Landscape and the human figure in repose—these are the symbols through which, in the past, the spiritual life has been most clearly and powerfully expressed, "Be still and know that I am God." Recollectedness is the indispensable means to the unitive knowledge of spiritual reality; and though recollectedness should and by some actually can be practised in the midst of the most violent physical activity, it is most effectively symbolized by a body in repose and a face that expresses an inner serenity. The carved or painted Buddhas and Bodhisattvas of

India and the Far East are perhaps the most perfect examples of such visual symbols of the spiritual life. Hardly less adequate are the majestic Byzantine figures of Christ, the Virgin and the Saints. It seems strange that El Greco, who received his first training from Byzantine masters, should not have recognized the symbolical value of repose, but should have preferred to represent or, through his accessory abstractions, to imply, an agitation wholly incompatible with the spiritual life of which he had read in the pages of Dionysius.

No less strange is the fact that a disciple of Titian should have ignored landscape and that a Neo-Platonist should have failed to perceive that, in the aged master's religious pictures, the only hint of spirituality was to be found, not in the all too human figures, but in the backgrounds of Alpine foothills, peaks and skies. Civilized man spends most of his life in a cosy little universe of material artefacts, of social conventions and of verbalized ideas. Only rarely, if he is in the inhabitant of a well-ordered city, does he come into direct contact with the mystery of the non-human world, does he become aware of modes of being incommensurable with his own, of vast, indefinite extensions, of durations all but everlasting. From time immemorial deity has been associated with the boundlessness of earth and sky, with the longevity of trees, rivers and mountains, with Leviathan and the whirlwind, with sunshine and the lilies of the field. Space and time on the cosmic scale are symbols of the infinity and eternity of Spirit. Non-human nature is the outward and visible expression of the mystery which confronts us when we look into the depths of our own being. The first artists to concern themselves with the spiritual significance of nature were the Taoist landscape painters of China. "Cherishing the Way, a virtuous man responds to objects. Clarifying his mind, a wise man appreciates forms. As to landscapes, they exist in material substance and soar into the realm of spirit. . . . The virtuous man follows the Way by spiritual insight; the wise man takes the same approach. But the lovers of landscape are led into the Way by a sense of form. . . . The significance which is too subtle to be communicated by means of word of mouth may be grasped by the mind through books and writings. Then how much more so in my case, when I have wandered among the rocks and hills and carefully observed them with my own eyes! I render form by form and appearance by appearance. . . . The truth comprises the expression received through the eyes and recognized by the mind. If, in painting, therefore, the likeness of an object is skilfully portrayed, both the eye and the mind will approve. When the eyes respond and the mind agrees with the objects, the divine spirit may be felt and truth may be attained in the painting." So wrote Tsung Ping, who was a contemporary of St. Augustine, in an Introduction to *Landscape Painting*, which has become a Chinese classic. When, twelve hundred years later, European artists discovered landscape, they developed no philosophy to explain and justify what they were doing. That was left to the poets—to Wordsworth, to Shelley, to Whitman. The Presence which they found in nature, "the Spirit of each spot," is identical with Hsuan P'in, the mysterious Valley Spirit of the Tao Te Ching, who reveals herself to the landscape painter and, by him, is revealed to others in his pictures. But the lack of an explanatory philosophy did not prevent the best of the European landscape painters from making manifest that

> "*Something far more deeply interfused,*
> *Whose dwelling is the light of setting suns,*
> *And the round ocean, and the living air,*
> *And the blue sky, and in the mind of man.*"

"This is not drawing," Blake exclaimed, when he was shown one of Constable's sketches, "this is inspiration." And though Constable himself protested that it was only drawing, the fact remains that the best of his landscapes are powerful and convincing renderings of the spiritual reality in which all things have their being. Indeed, they are much more adequate as symbols of spiritual life than the majority of the works in which Blake consciously tried to express his spiritualist philosophy. Much less gifted as painter than as poet, and brought up in a deplorable artistic tradition, Blake rarely produced a picture that 'comes off' to the extent of expressing what he says so perfectly in his lyrics and in isolated passages of the Prophetic Books. Constable, on the other hand, is a great nature mystic without knowing or intending it. In this he reminds us of Seurat. "They see poetry in what I do," complained that consummate master of landscape. "No; I apply my method and that is all there is to it." But the method was applied by a painter who combined the most exquisite sensibility with intellectual powers of the first order. Consequently what Seurat supposed to be merely *pointillisme* was in fact inspiration—was a vision of the world in which material reality is the symbol and, one might say, the incarnation of an all-embracing spiritual reality. The famous method was the means whereby he told this Taostic and Wordsworthian story; *pointillisme*, as he used it, permitted him to render empty space as no other painter has ever done, and to impose, through colour, an unprecedented degree of unity upon his composition. In Seurat's paintings the near and the far are separate and yet are one. The emptiness which is the symbol of infinity is of the same substance as the finite forms it contains. The transient participates in the eternal, *samsara* and *nirvana* are one and the same. Such is the poetry with which, in spite of himself, Seurat filled those wonderful landscapes of Honfleur and Gravelines and the Seine. And such is the poetry which El Greco, in spite of what seems to have been a conscious desire to imply it, was forced by the nature of his artistic instrument to exclude from every picture he painted. His peculiar treatment of space and form tells a story of obscure happenings in the sub-conscious mind—of some haunting fear of wide vistas and the open air, some dream of security in the imagined equivalent of a womb. The conscious aspiration towards union with, and perfect freedom in, the divine spirit is overridden by a sub-conscious longing for the consolations of some ineffable uterine state. In these paintings there is no redemption of time by eternity, no transfiguration of matter by the spirit. On the contrary, it is the low-level organic that has engulfed the spiritual and transformed it into its own substance.

When we think of it in relation to the great world of human experience, El Greco's universe of swallowed spirit and visceral rapture seems, as I have said, curiously oppressive and disquieting. But considered as an isolated artistic system, how strong and coherent it seems, how perfectly unified, how fascinatingly beautiful! And because of this inner harmony and coherence, it asserts in one way all that it had denied in another. El Greco's conscious purpose was to affirm man's capacity for union with the divine. Unconsciously, by his choice of forms and his peculiar treatment of space, he proclaimed the triumph of the organic and the incapacity of spirit, so far as he personally was concerned, to transfigure the matter with which it is associated. But at the same time he was a painter of genius. Out of the visceral forms and cramped spaces, imposed upon him by a part of his being beyond his voluntary control, he was able to create a new kind of order and perfection and, through this order and perfection, to re-affirm the possibility of man's union with the Spirit—a possibility which the raw materials of his pictures had seemed to rule out.

There is no question here of a dialectical process of thesis, antithesis and synthesis. A work of art is not a becoming, but a multiple being. It exists and has significance on several levels at once. In most cases these significances are of the same kind and harmoniously reinforce one another. Not always, however. Occasionally it happens that each of the meanings is logically exclusive of all the rest. There is then a happy marriage of incompatibles, a perfect fusion of contradictions. It is one of those states which, though inconceivable, actually occur. Such things cannot be; and yet, when you enter the Prado, when you visit Toledo, there they actually are.

VARIATIONS ON *THE PRISONS*

AT the top of the main staircase in University College, London, there stands a box-like structure of varnished wood, somewhat larger than a telephone booth, somewhat smaller than an outdoor privy. When the door of this miniature house is opened, a light goes on inside, and those who stand upon the threshold find themselves confronted by a little old gentleman sitting bolt upright in a chair and smiling benevolently into space. His hair is grey and hangs almost to his shoulders; his wide-brimmed straw hat is like something out of the illustrations to an early edition of *Paul et Virginie*; he wears a cutaway coat (green, if I remember rightly, with metal buttons) and pantaloons of white cotton, discreetly striped. This little old gentleman is Jeremy Bentham, or at least what remains of Jeremy Bentham after the dissection ordered in his will—a skeleton with hands and face of wax, dressed in the clothes which once belonged to the author of *The Principles of Morals and Legislation*.

To this odd shrine (so characteristic, in its excessive unpretentiousness, of "that nook-shotten isle of Albion") I paid my visit of curiosity in the company of one of the most extraordinary, one of the most admirable men of our time, Dr. Albert Schweitzer. Many years have passed since then; but I remember very clearly the expression of affectionate amusement which appeared on Schweitzer's face as he looked at the mummy. "Dear Bentham," he said at last, "dear Bentham! I like him so much better than Hegel. He was responsible for so much less harm."

The comment was unexpected but true, and, in our twentieth-century context, painfully to the point. The German philosopher was proud of being *tief*, but lacked completely the humility which is the necessary condition of the ultimate profundity. That was why he ended up as the idolater of the Prussian state and the spiritual father of those Marxian theories of history, in terms of which it is possible to justify every atrocity on the part of true believers and to condemn every good or reasonable act performed by infidels. Bentham, on the contrary, made no claims to *tief*ness. Shallow with the kindly and sensible shallowness of the eighteenth century, he thought of individuals as real people, not as mere cells in the brawn and bone of a social organism, whose soul is the State. From Hegel's depths have sprung tyranny, war and persecutions; from the shallows of Bentham, a host of unpretentious but real benefits—the repeal of antiquated laws, the introduction of sewage systems, the reform of municipal government, almost everything sensible and humane in the civilization of the nineteenth century. Only in one field did Bentham ever sow the teeth of dragons. He had the logician's passion for order and consistency; and he wanted to impose his ideas of tidiness not only upon thoughts and words, but also upon things and institutions. Now tidiness is undeniably a good—but a good of which it is easily possible to have too much and at too high a price. The love of tidiness has often figured, along with the love of power, as an incitement to tyranny. In human affairs the extreme of messiness is anarchy; the extreme of tidiness, an army or a penitentiary. Anarchy is the enemy of liberty, and so, at its highest pitch, is mechanical efficiency. The good life can be lived only in a society where tidiness is preached and practised, but not too fanatically, and where efficiency is always haloed, as it were, by a tolerated aura of mess. Bentham himself was no tyrant and no worshipper of the all-efficient, ubiquitous and providential State. But he loved tidiness and inculcated that kind of social efficiency which has been and is being made an excuse for the concentration of power in the hands of a few experts and the regimentation of the masses. And meanwhile we have to remember the strange and rather alarming fact that Bentham devoted about twenty-five years of his long life to the elaboration in minutest detail of the plans for a perfectly efficient prison. The Panopticon, as he called it, was to be a circular building so constructed that every convict should pass his life in perpetual solitude while remaining under the perpetual surveillance of a warder posted at the centre. (Significantly enough, Jeremy Bentham borrowed the idea of the Panopticon from his brother, Sir Samuel, the naval architect, who, while employed by Catherine the Great to build warships for Russia, had designed a factory along panoptical lines, for the purpose of getting more work out of the newly industrialized *mujiks*.) Bentham's plan for a totalitarian housing project was never carried out. To console him for his disappointment, the philosopher was granted, by Act of Parliament, twenty-three thousand pounds from the public funds.

The architecture of modern prisons lacks the logical perfection of the Panopticon; but its inspiration is that same passion for a more than human tidiness which moved the Bentham brothers and which has been, time out of mind, characteristic of martinets and dictators. Before the days of Howard and Bentham and the Philadelphia Quakers, nobody, for some odd reason, seems ever to have thought of making prisons orderly and efficient. The gaols to which Elizabeth Fry brought her inexhaustible treasures of charity and common sense were like the embodiments of some criminal delirium. Passing those doors, the prisoner found himself condemned to an existence resembling that of Hobbes's theoretical state of nature. Behind the façade of Newgate—a façade which its architect, uninhibited by the tiresome necessity of finding a place for windows, had been able to make consummately elegant—there existed, not a world of men and women, not even a world of beasts, but a chaos, a pandemonium.

The artist whose work most faithfully reflects the nature of this hell is Hogarth—not the Hogarth of the harmoniously coloured paintings, but he of the engravings, he of the hard insensitive line, the ruthless delineator of senseless evil and chaotic misery, as well within the Fleet and Newgate and Bedlam as outside, in those other prisons, those other asylums, the dram-shops of Gin Alley, the brothels and gaming-rooms of Covent Garden, the suburban playgrounds, where children torment their dogs and birds with scarcely imaginable refinements of cruelty and obscenity.

Within a space of thirty or forty years the Prison Discipline Society accomplished an extraordinary reformation. From being sub-humanly anarchical, prisons became sub-humanly mechanical. Ever since Sir Joshua Jebb erected his model gaol at Pentonville, the consciousness of being inside a machine, inside a realized idea of absolute tidiness and perfect regimentation, has been a principal part of the punishment of convicts. In the Nazi concentration camps hell on earth was not of the old Hogarthian kind, but neat, tidy, thoroughly scientific. Seen from the air, Belsen is said to have looked like an atomic research laboratory or a well-designed motion picture studio. The Bentham brothers have been dead these hundred years and more; but the spirit of the Panopticon, the spirit of Sir Samuel's *mujik*-compelling workhouse, has gone marching on to strange and terrible destinations.

Today every efficient office, every up-to-date factory is a panoptical prison, in which the worker suffers (more or less, according to the character of the warders and the degree of his own sensibility) from the consciousness of being inside a machine. It is, I think, only in literature that there has been an adequate artistic rendering of this consciousness. De Vigny, for example, has said fine and penetrating things about the soldier's enslavement to an ideal of absolute tidiness; and in *War and Peace* there is a memorable chapter on the way in which the impersonal forces of Orders from Above, of High Policy expressing itself through the workings of a system, transforms Pierre's kindly French gaolers into insensitive and pitiless automata. But in the twentieth century an army is only one among many Panopticons. There are also the regiments of industry, the regiments of book-keeping and administration. These have evoked a good deal of plaintive or truculent writing, but not much, and nothing very satisfactory, in the way of pictorial art. There were, it is true, certain Cubists, who liked to paint machines or to represent human figures as though they were parts of machines. But a machine, after all, is itself a work of art, much more subtle, much more interesting from a formal point of view, than any representation of a machine can be. In other words, a machine is its own highest artistic expression and merely loses by being simplified and quintessentialized in a symbolic representation. As for the representation of human beings in mechanomorphic guise—this is effective only to a certain point. For the real horror of the situation in an industrial or administrative Panopticon is not that human beings are transformed into machines (if they could be so transformed, they would be perfectly happy in their prisons); no, the horror consists precisely in the fact that they are not machines, but freedom-loving animals, far-ranging minds and God-like spirits, who find themselves subordinated to machines and constrained to live within the issueless tunnel of an arbitrary and inhuman system.

Beyond the real historical prisons of too much tidiness and those where anarchy engenders the hell of physical and moral chaos, there lie yet other prisons, no less terrible for being fantastic and unembodied—the metaphysical prisons, whose seat is within the mind, whose walls are made of nightmare and incomprehension, whose chains are anxiety and their racks a sense of personal and even generic guilt. De Quincey's Oxford Street and the road on which he had his vision of sudden death were prisons of this kind. So was the luxurious inferno described by Beckford in *Vathek*. So were the castles, the court-rooms, the penal colonies inhabited by the personages of Kafka's novels. And, passing from the world of words to that of forms, we find these same metaphysical prisons delineated with incomparable force in the strangest and, in many ways, the most beautiful, of Piranesi's etchings.

Historical generalizations are delightful to make and thrilling to read. But how much, I wonder, do they contribute to our understanding of the human enigma? The question is one which I will not venture to answer, except with a series of other questions. For example, if, as we are told, the art of a period reflects the social history of that period, in what way precisely do Perugino's paintings express the age whose history is written in *The Prince* of Machiavelli? Again, modern historians assure us that the thirteenth century was the Age of Faith and a period of progress. Then why should all the moralists who actually lived during the thirteenth century have regarded it as an age of decadence and why should its liveliest chronicler, Salimbene, depict for us a society that behaves as though it had never even heard of Christian morals? Or consider the fourth century in Constantinople. At this time and place, we are assured by certain historians, men were wholly preoccupied with problems of theology. If this is the case, why do the writers who were contemporary with those men complain that they lived only for the chariot races? And, finally, why should Voltaire and Hume be regarded as more typical of the eighteenth century than Bach and Wesley? Why have I myself, in an earlier paragraph, spoken of the kindly and sensible shallowness of the eighteenth century, when that century gave birth to such men as William Law and Saint-Martin, to the author of the *Songs of Experience* and the engraver of *The Prisons*. The truth is, of course, that every variety of human being exists at every period. In religion, for example, every generation has its fetishists, its revival-

A Prison. *From an engraving by Piranesi*

Jeremy Bentham. *By H. W. Pickersgill*

ists, its legalists, its rationalists and its mystics. And, whatever the prevailing fashion in art may happen to be, every age has its congenital romantics and its natural classicists. True, at any period the prevailing fashions in art, in religion, in modes of thought and feeling are more or less rigid. Consequently it is always more or less hard for those, whose temperaments are at odds with the fashion, to express themselves. Any given work of art may be represented as the diagonal in a parallelogram of forces—a parallelogram of which the base is the prevailing tradition and the socially important events of the time, and in which the upright is the artist's temperament and his private life. In some works the base is longer than the upright; in others the upright is longer than the base.

Piranesi's *Prisons* are creations of the second kind. In them the personal, private and therefore universal and everlasting upright is notably longer than the merely historical and therefore transient and local base. The proof of this is to be found in the fact that these extraordinary etchings have continued, during two centuries, to seem completely relevant and modern, not merely in their formal aspects, but also as expressions of obscure psychological truths. To use a once popular religious phrase, they "spoke to the condition" of Coleridge and De Quincey and they speak no less eloquently to ours. That which Piranesi expressed is not subject to historical change. He is not, like Hogarth, recording the facts of contemporary social life. Nor is he, like Bentham, trying to design a mechanism that shall change the nature of such facts. His concern is with states of the soul—states that are largely independent of external circumstances, states that recur whenever Nature, at her everlasting game of chance, combines the hereditary factors of physique and temperament in certain patterns.

In the past psychology was generally treated as a branch of ethics or theology. Thus, for St. Augustine, the problem of human differences was the same as the problem of Grace and the mystery of God's Good Pleasure. And it is only in quite recent times that men have learnt to talk about the idiosyncrasies of personal behaviour in any terms but those of sin and virtue. The metaphysical prisons delineated by Piranesi, and described by so many modern poets and novelists, were well known to our ancestors—but well known, not as symptoms of disease or of some temperamental peculiarity, not as states to be analysed and expressed by lyric poets, but rather as moral imperfections, as criminal rebellions against God, as obstacles in the way of enlightenment. Thus the *weltschmerz*, of which the German Romantics were so proud, the *ennui*, *fruit de la morne incuriosité*, which was the theme of so many of Baudelaire's most splendid verses, is nothing else than that *acedia*, for indulging in which the constitutionally bored and melancholy were plunged head over ears in the black mud of hell's third circle. And this is what St. Catherine of Siena had to say about the state of mind which is the very climate and atmosphere of all Kafka's novels. "Confusion is a leprosy that dries up body and soul, and binds the arms of holy desire. It makes the soul unendurable to itself, disposing the mind to conflicts and fantasies. It robs the soul of supernatural light and darkens its natural light. Let the demons of confusion be vanquished by living faith and holy desire." To someone like St. Catherine, whose primary concern was union with God and the salvation of souls, even to someone whose preoccupation with Christianity was, like Dante's, rather that of a philosopher than of a theocentric saint, the idea of treating spiritual confusion or *acedia* or any other kind of metaphysical prison as merely a subject for scientific research or artistic manipulation would have seemed a kind of criminal imbecility. The historical base upon which mediaeval thinkers and artists erected their personal uprights was so long and so deeply rooted in traditional theology and ethics, that it proved impossible even for Boccaccio—born story-teller and passionate humanist though he was—to pay more than the most perfunctory attention to psychology. In the *Decameron* even the outward appearance of the personages is hardly described; and the characterization is confined to simple adjectives, such as 'gentle,' 'courtly,' 'avaricious,' 'amorous' and the like. It required a greater genius and a profounder scepticism than Boccaccio's to invent a psychology independent of theology and ethics. And let us remember that Chaucer—the Chaucer of the later *Canterbury Tales*—remained without any rival until the time of Shakespeare. In relation to its traditional base, his personal upright is the tallest in all mediaeval literature. The resulting diagonal represents a work of truly astounding originality.

On their much smaller scale *The Prisons* of Piranesi are also astonishingly original. No previous painter or draughtsmen had ever done anything at all like them. There had, of course, been plenty of fantasists before the days of Piranesi—even fantasists who expressed themselves in terms of architectural design, like the Bibbienas. But the Bibbienas were men of the theatre and their architectural inventions were intended primarily to astonish the groundlings, to express, not the subterranean workings of a tormented soul, but those thoroughly vulgar aspirations towards grandiosity which, throughout the seventeenth and eighteenth centuries, tormented the great ones of the earth, together with all who snobbishly wanted to be like them. Another, more celebrated fantasist was Salvator Rosa—a man who, for reasons which are now incomprehensible, was regarded by the critics of four and five generations ago as one of the world's greatest artists. But Salvator Rosa's romantic fantasies are pretty cheap and obvious. He is a melodramatist who never penetrates beneath the surface. If he were alive today, he would be known, most probably, as the indefatigable author of one of the more bloodthirsty and uninhibited comic strips. Much more talented was Magnasco, whose speciality was monks by candlelight in a state of Gothic or Greco-esque elongation. His inventions are always pleasing, but always, one feels, without any deep or abiding significance—things created arbitrarily on one of the higher levels of consciousness, somewhere near the top of a very whimsical and accomplished head. The fantasy displayed in *The Prisons* is altogether of a different order. It is a fantasy without precedent, based upon facts, which Piranesi was the first to describe in pictorial terms. All the plates in the series are self-evidently variations on a single symbol, whose reference is to things existing in the physical and metaphysical depths of human souls and bodies—to *acedia* and confusion, to nightmare and *angst*, to incomprehension and panic bewilderment.

The most disquietingly obvious fact about all these dungeons is the perfect pointlessness which reigns throughout. Their architecture is colossal and magnificent. One is made to feel that the genius of great artists and the labour of innumerable slaves have gone into the creation of these monuments, every detail of which is completely without a purpose. Yes, without a purpose; for the staircases lead nowhere, the vaults support nothing but their own weight and enclose vast spaces that are never truly rooms, but only ante-rooms, lumber-rooms, vestibules, outhouses. And this magnificence of cyclopean stone is everywhere made squalid by wooden ladders, by flimsy gangways and catwalks. And the squalor is for squalor's sake, since all these rickety roads through space are manifestly without destination. Below them, on the floor, stand great machines incapable of doing anything in particular, and from the arches overhead hang ropes that carry nothing except a sickening suggestion of torture. Some of the prisons are lighted only by narrow windows. Others are half open to the sky, with hints of yet other vaults and walls in the distance. But even where the enclosure is more or less complete, Piranesi always contrives to give the impression that this colossal pointlessness goes on indefinitely and is co-extensive with the universe. Engaged in no recognizable activity, paying no attention to one another, a few small faceless figures haunt the shadows. Their insignificant presence merely emphasizes the fact that there is nobody at home.

Physically, every human being is always alone, suffering in solitude, enjoying in solitude, incapable of participating in the vital processes of his fellows. But, though self-contained, this island organism is never self-sufficient. Each living solitude is dependent upon other living solitudes and, more completely still, upon the ocean of being from which it lifts its tiny reef of individuality. The realization of this paradox of solitude in the midst of dependence, of isolation accompanied by insufficiency, is one of the principal causes of confusion and *acedia* and anxiety. And in their turn, of course, confusion and *acedia* and anxiety intensify the sense of loneliness and make the human paradox seem yet more tragic. The occupants of these metaphysical prisons are the hopeless spectators of "this pomp of worlds, this pain of birth"—of a magnificence without meaning, a misery without end and beyond the power of unaided man to understand or to bear.

It is said that the first idea of *The Prisons* came to Piranesi in the delirium of fever. What is certain, however, is that this first idea was not the last; for some of the etchings exist in early states, in which many of the most characteristic and most disquieting details of *The Prisons*, as we now know them, are lacking. From this it is to be inferred that the state of mind expressed in these etchings was, for Piranesi, chronic and in some sort normal. Fever may have originally suggested *The Prisons*; but in the years which elapsed between Piranesi's first essays and the final publication of the plates, recurrent moods of confusion and *acedia* and *angst* must have been responsible for such obscure but, as we now see, indispensable symbols as the ropes, the aimless engines, the makeshift wooden stairs and bridges.

The plates of *The Prisons* were published while their author was still a young man, and during the remainder of his fairly long life Piranesi never returned to the theme which, in them, he had handled with such consummate mastery. Most of his work, thenceforward, was topographical and archaeological. His theme was always Rome; and this was true even when he abandoned the facts of ruins and baroque churches to undertake excursions into the realm of fantasy. For what he liked to imagine was still Rome—Rome as it ought to have been, as it might have been, if Augustus and his successors had possessed an inexhaustible treasury and an inexhaustible supply of man-power. It is fortunate that their resources were limited; for the hypothetical Rome of Piranesi's fancy and the imperial dreams is a nightmare of pretentiousness and grandiose vulgarity.

St. Catherine held that the demons of confusion are to be vanquished only by holy desire and faith in the Christian revelation. But actually any sustained desire and any intense faith will win the battle. Piranesi seems to have been without any profound religious conviction or mystical aspiration. His faith was that of a humanist, his god was Roman antiquity and his motivating desire was a mixture of the artist's will to beauty, the archaeologist's will to historical truth and the poor man's will to make a living for his family. These, apparently, were sufficient antidotes to *acedia* and spiritual confusion. At any rate he never gave a second expression to the state of mind which inspired *The Prisons*.

Considered from a purely formal point of view, *The Prisons* are remarkable as being the nearest eighteenth-century approach to a purely abstract art. The raw material of Piranesi's designs consists of architectural forms; but, because *The Prisons* are images of confusion, because their essence is pointlessness, the combinations of architectural forms never add up to an architectural drawing, but remain free designs, untrammelled by any considerations of utility or even of possibility, and limited only by the necessity of evoking the general idea of a building. In other words, Piranesi uses architectural forms to produce a series of beautifully intricate designs, which resemble the abstractions of the Cubists in being composed of geometrical elements, but which have the advantage of combining pure geometry with enough subject-matter, enough literature, to express more forcibly than a mere pattern can do, the obscure and terrible states of spiritual confusion and *acedia*.

Of natural, as opposed to geometrical, forms Piranesi, in *The Prisons*, makes hardly any use. There is not a leaf or a blade of grass in the whole series, not a bird or an animal. Here and there, irrelevantly alive in the midst of the stony abstractions, stand a few human figures, darkly cloaked, featureless and impassive.

In the topographical etchings things are very different. Here Piranesi uses natural forms as a romantically decorative foil to the pure geometry of the monuments. The trees have an unkempt wildness; the personages in the foreground are either beggars, inconceivably ragged, or else fine ladies and gentlemen no less inconceivably beribboned and be-wigged, sometimes on foot, sometimes in rococo coaches, carved into the likeness of wedding-cakes or merry-go-rounds. Everywhere the purpose is to set off the smoothness and solidity of hewn stone by juxtaposing the wavering, flame-like forms of plants and human beings. At the same time the figures serve another purpose, which is to make the monuments seem larger than in fact they are. Men and women are reduced to the stature of children; horses become as small as mastiffs.

Inside the basilicas the pious reach up to the holy water fonts and, even on tiptoe, can hardly wet their fingers. Peopled by dwarfs, the most modest of baroque buildings assumes heroic proportions; a little piece of classicism by Pietro da Cortona seems gravely portentous, and the delightful gimcrack of Borromini takes on the quality of something cyclopean. This trick of increasing the apparent size of buildings by diminishing the known yardstick of the human figure was a favourite device among eighteenth-century artists. It was reduced to its final absurdity in such pictures as the *Belshazzar's Feast* of John Martin, where the ant-like king and his courtiers sit down to dinner in a hall about two miles long and fifteen hundred feet high.

In *The Prisons* there is no hint of this ingenuous and simple-minded theatricality. Such prisoners as we are shown exist for the purpose of emphasizing, not the super-human grandeur of the buildings, but their inhuman vacancy, their sub-human pointlessness. They are, quite literally, lost souls, wandering—or not even wandering, standing about—in a labyrinthine emptiness. It is interesting to compare them with the personages in Blake's illustrations to the *Inferno* of Dante. These damned souls are so far from being lost that they seem to be perfectly at home among their flames and crags and morasses. In all the circles of hell everybody is vaguely heroic in the corrupt classical manner of the late eighteenth century, and everybody appears to take the liveliest interest in his fellows. In *The Prisons* there are no Michelangelesque muscles, no exhibitionism of athletic extraverts, no trace of social life and no hint that such a thing is even possible. Every man is muffled up, furtive and, even when in company, completely alone. Blake's drawings are curious and sometimes beautiful; but never for a moment can we take them seriously as symbols of extremist suffering. Piranesi's prisoners, on the contrary, are the inhabitants of a hell which, though but one out of the many worst of all possible worlds, is completely credible and bears the stamp of self-evident authenticity.

VARIATIONS ON GOYA

THERE are anthologies of almost everything—from the best to the worst, from the historically significant to the eccentric, from the childish to the sublime. But there is one anthology, potentially the most interesting of them all, which, to the best of my knowledge, has never yet been compiled; I mean, the Anthology of Later Works.

To qualify for inclusion in such an anthology, the artist would have to pass several tests. First of all, he must have avoided a premature extinction and lived on into artistic and chronological maturity. Thus the last poems of Shelley, the last compositions of Schubert and even of Mozart would find no place in our collection. Consummate artists as they were, these men were still psychologically youthful when they died. For their full development they needed more time than their earthly destiny allowed them. Of a different order are those strange beings whose chronological age is out of all proportion to their maturity, not only as artists, but as human spirits. Thus, some of the letters written by Keats in his early twenties and many of the paintings which Seurat executed before his death at thirty-two might certainly qualify as Later Works. But, as a general rule, a certain minimum of time is needed for the ripening of such fruits. For the most part, our hypothetical antholo-

This essay was published originally as the foreword to *The Complete Etchings of Goya* (Crown Publishers, New York, 1943).

gist will make his selections from the art of elderly and middle-aged men and women.

But by no means all middle-aged and elderly artists are capable of producing significant Later Works. For the last half-century of a long life, Wordsworth preserved an almost unbroken record of dullness. And in this respect he does not stand alone. There are many, many others whose Later Works are their worst. All these must be excluded from our anthology, and I would pass a similar judgment on that other large class of Later Works, which, though up to the standard of the earlier, are not significantly different from them. Haydn lived to a ripe old age and his right hand never forgot its cunning; but it also failed to learn a new cunning. Peter Pan-like, he continued, as an old man, to write the same sort of thing he had written twenty, thirty and forty years before. Where there is nothing to distinguish the creations of a man's maturity from those of his youth it is superfluous to include any of them in a selection of characteristically Later Works.

This leaves us, then, with the Later Works of those artists who have lived without ever ceasing to learn of life. The field is relatively narrow; but within it, what astonishing, and sometimes what disquieting treasures! One thinks of the ineffable serenity of the slow movement of Beethoven's A Minor Quartet, the peace passing all understanding of the orchestral prelude to the *Benedictus* of his *Missa Solemnis*. But this is not the old man's only mood; when he turns from the contemplation of eternal reality to a consideration of the human world, we are treated to the positively terrifying merriment of the last movement of his B Flat Major Quartet—merriment quite inhuman, peals of violent and yet somehow abstract laughter echoing down from somewhere beyond the limits of the world. Of the same nature, but if possible even more disquieting, is the mirth which reverberates through the last act of Verdi's *Falstaff*, culminating in that extraordinary final chorus in which the aged genius makes his maturest comment on the world—not with bitterness or sarcasm or satire, but in a huge, contrapuntal paroxysm of detached and already posthumous laughter.

Turning to the other arts, we find something of the same non-human, posthumous quality in the Later Works of Yeats and, coupled with a prodigious majesty, in those of Piero della Francesca. And then, of course, there is *The Tempest*—a work charged with something of the unearthly serenity of Beethoven's *Benedictus* but concluding in the most disappointing anticlimax, with Prospero giving up his magic for the sake (heaven help us!) of becoming once again a duke. And the same sort of all too human anticlimax saddens us at the end of the second part of *Faust*, with its implication that draining fens is Man's Final End, and that the achievement of this end automatically qualifies the drainer for the beatific vision.

And what about the last El Grecos—for example, that unimaginable *Immaculate Conception* at Toledo with its fantastic harmony of brilliant, ice-cold colours, its ecstatic gesticulations in a heaven with a third dimension no greater than that of a mine-shaft, its deliquescence of flesh and flowers and drapery into a set of ectoplasmic abstractions? What about them, indeed? All we know is that, beautiful and supremely enigmatic, they will certainly take their place in our hypothetical anthology.

And finally, among these and all other extraordinary Later Works, we should have to number the paintings, drawings and etchings of Goya's final twenty-five or thirty years.

The difference between the young Goya and the old may be best studied and appreciated by starting in the basement of the Prado, where his cartoons for the tapestries are hung; climbing thence to the main floor, where there is a room full of his portraits of royal imbeciles, grandees, enchanting duchesses, majas, clothed and unclothed; walking thence to the smaller room containing those two great paintings: the Second of May—Napoleon's Mamelukes cutting down the crowd—and *Los Fusilamientos del Tres de Mayo*, the firing squads at work upon their victims by the light of lanterns; and finally, mounting to the top floor where hang the etchings and drawings, together with those unutterably mysterious and disturbing 'black paintings,' with which the deaf and ageing Goya elected to adorn the dining-room of his house, the Quinta del Sordo. It is a progress from light-hearted eighteenth-century art, hardly at all unconventional in subject-matter or in handling, through fashionable brilliancy and increasing virtuosity to something quite timeless both in technique and spirit—the most powerful of commentaries on human crime and madness, made in terms of an artistic convention uniquely fitted to express precisely that extraordinary mingling of hatred and compassion, despair and sardonic humour, realism and fantasy.

"I show you sorrow," said the Buddha, "and the ending of sorrow"—the sorrow of the phenomenal world in which man, "like an angry ape, plays such fantastic tricks before high heaven as make the angels weep," and the ending of sorrow in the beatific vision, the unitive contemplation of transcendental reality. Apart from the fact that he is a great and, one might say, uniquely original artist, Goya is significant as being, in his Later Works, the almost perfect type of the man who knows only sorrow and not the ending of sorrow.

In spite of his virulent anti-clericalism, Goya contrived to remain on sufficiently good terms with the Church to receive periodical commissions to paint religious pictures. Some of these, like the frescoes in the cupola of La Florida, are frankly and avowedly secular. But others are serious essays in religious painting. It is worth looking rather closely at what is probably the best of these religious pieces—the fine *Agony in the Garden*. With outstretched arms, Christ raises towards the comforting angel a face whose expression is identical with that of the poor creatures whom we see, in a number of unforgettably painful etchings and paintings, kneeling or standing in an excruciating anticipation before the gun-barrels of a French firing squad. There is no trace here of that loving confidence which, even in the darkest hours, fills the hearts of men and women who live continually in the presence of God; not so much as a hint of what François de Sales calls 'holy indifference' to suffering and good fortune, of the fundamental equanimity, the peace passing all understanding, which belongs to those whose attention is firmly fixed upon a transcendental reality.

For Goya the transcendental reality did not exist. There is no evidence in his biography or his works that he ever had even the most distant personal experience of it. The only reality he knew was that of the world around him; and the longer he lived the more frightful did that world seem—the more frightful, that is to say, in the eyes of his rational self; for his animal high spirits went on bubbling up irrepressibly, whenever his body was free from pain or sickness, to the very end. As a young man in good health, with money and reputation, a fine position and as many women as he wanted, he had found the world a very agreeable place. Absurd, of course, and with enough of folly and roguery to furnish subject-matter for innumerable satirical drawings, but eminently worth living in. Then all of a sudden came deafness; and, after the joyful dawn of the Revolution, Napoleon and French Imperialism and the atrocities of war; and, when Napoleon's hordes were gone, the unspeakable Ferdinand VII and clerical reaction and the spectacle of Spaniards fighting among themselves; and all the time, like the drone of a bagpipe accompanying the louder noises of what is officially called history, the enormous stupidity of average men and women, the chronic squalor of their superstitions, the bestiality of their occasional violences and orgies.

Realistically or in fantastic allegories, with a technical mastery that only increased as he grew older, Goya recorded it all. Not only the agonies endured by his people at the hands of the invaders, but also the follies and crimes committed by these same people in their dealings with one another. The great canvases of the Madrid massacres and executions, the incomparable etchings of War's Disasters, fill us with an indignant compassion. But then we turn to the *Disparates* and the *Pinturas Negras*. In these, with a sublimely impartial savagery, Goya sets down exactly what he thinks of the martyrs of the *Dos*

The 2nd of May 1808. *By Goya*

The 3rd of May 1808. *By Goya*

de Mayo when they are not being martyred. Here, for example, are two men—two Spaniards—sinking slowly towards death in an engulfing quicksand, but busily engaged in knocking one another over the head with bludgeons. And here is a rabble coming home from a pilgrimage—scores of low faces, distorted as though by reflection in the back of a spoon, all open-mouthed and yelling. And all the blank black eyes stare vacantly and idiotically in different directions.

These creatures who haunt Goya's Later Works are inexpressibly horrible, with the horror of mindlessness and animality and spiritual darkness. And above the lower depths where they obscenely pullulate is a world of bad priests and lustful friars, of fascinating women whose love is a "dream of lies and inconstancy," of fatuous nobles and, at the top of the social pyramid, a royal family of half-wits, sadists, Messalinas and perjurers. The moral of it all is summed up in the central plate of the *Caprichos*, in which we see Goya himself, his head on his arms, sprawled across his desk and fitfully sleeping, while the air above is peopled with the bats and owls of necromancy and just behind his chair lies an enormous witch's cat, malevolent as only Goya's cats can be, staring at the sleeper with baleful eyes. On the side of the desk are traced the words, "The dream of reason produces monsters." It is a caption that admits of more than one interpretation. When Reason sleeps, the absurd and loathsome creatures of superstition wake and are active, goading their victim to an ignoble frenzy. But this is not all, Reason may also dream without sleeping; may intoxicate itself, as it did during the French Revolution, with the day-dreams of inevitable progress, of liberty, equality and fraternity imposed by violence, of human self-sufficiency and the ending of sorrow, not by the all too arduous method which alone offers any prospect of success, but by political re-arrangements and a better technology. The *Caprichos* were published in the last year of the eighteenth century; in 1808 Goya and all Spain were given the opportunity of discovering the consequences of such day-dreaming. Murat marched his troops into Madrid; the *Desastres de la Guerra* were about to begin.

Goya produced four main sets of etchings—the *Caprichos*, the *Desastres de la Guerra*, the *Tauromaquia* and the *Disparates* or *Proverbios*. All of them are Later Works. The *Caprichos* were not published until he was fifty-three; the plates of the *Desastres* were etched between the ages of sixty-five and seventy-five; the *Tauromaquia* series first saw the light when he was sixty-nine (and at the age of almost eighty he learned the brand new technique of lithography in order to be able to do justice to his beloved bulls in yet another medium); the *Disparates* were finished when he was seventy-three.

For the non-Spaniard the plates of the *Tauromaquia* series will probably seem the least interesting of Goya's etchings. They are brilliant records of the exploits of the bull-ring; but unfortunately, or fortunately, most of us know very little about bull-fighting. Consequently, we miss the finer shades of the significance of these little masterpieces of documentary art. Moreover, being documentary, the etchings of the *Tauromaquia* do not lend themselves to being executed with that splendid audacity, that dramatic breadth of treatment, which delight us in the later paintings and the etchings of the other three series. True, we find in this collection a few plates that are as fine as anything Goya ever produced—for example, that wonderful etching of the bull which has broken out of the arena and stands triumphant, a corpse hanging limp across its horns, among the spectators' benches. But by and large it is not to the *Tauromaquia* that we turn for the very best specimens of Goya's work in black and white, or for the most characteristic expressions of his mature personality. The nature of the subject-matter makes it impossible for him, in these plates, to reveal himself fully either as a man or as an artist.

Of the three other sets of etchings two, the *Caprichos* and *Disparates*, are fantastic and allegorical in subject-matter, while the third, the *Desastres*, though for the most part it represents real happenings under the Napoleonic terror, represents them in a way which, being generalized and symbolical, rather than directly documentary, permits of, and indeed demands, a treatment no less broad and dramatic than is given to the fantasies of the other collections.

War always weakens and often completely shatters the crust of customary decency which constitutes a civilization. It is a thin crust at the best of times, and beneath it lies—what? Look through Goya's *Desastres* and find out. The abyss of bestiality and diabolism and suffering seems almost bottomless. There is practically nothing of which human beings are not capable when war or revolution or anarchy gives them the necessary opportunity and excuse; and to their pain death alone imposes a limit.

Goya's record of disaster has a number of recurrent themes. There are those shadowy archways, for example, more sinister than those even of Piranesi's *Prisons*, where women are violated, captives squat in a hopeless stupor, corpses lie rotting, emaciated children starve to death. Then there are the vague street corners at which the famine-stricken hold out their hands; but the whiskered French hussars and carabiniers look on without pity, and even the rich Spaniards pass by indifferently, as though they were "of another lineage." Of still more frequent occurrence in the series are the crests of those naked hillocks on which lie the dead, like so much garbage. Or else, in dramatic silhouette against the sky above those same hill-tops, we see the hideous butchery of Spanish men and women, and the no less hideous vengeance meted out by infuriated Spaniards upon their tormentors. Often the hillock sprouts a single tree, always low, sometimes maimed by gun-fire. Upon its branches are impaled, like the beetles and caterpillars in a butcher bird's larder, whole naked torsos, sometimes decapitated, sometimes without arms; or else a pair of amputated legs, or a severed head—warnings, set there by the conquerors, of the fate awaiting those who dare oppose the Emperor. At other times the tree is used as a gallows—a less efficient gallows, indeed, than that majestic oak which, in Callot's *Misères de la Guerre*, is fruited with more than a score of swinging corpses, but good enough for a couple of executions *en passant*, except, of course, in the case recorded in one of Goya's most hair-raising plates, in which the tree is too stumpy to permit of a man's hanging clear of the ground. But the rope is fixed, none the less, and to tighten the noose around their victim's neck, two French soldiers tug at the legs, while with his foot a third man thrusts with all his strength against the shoulders.

And so the record proceeds, horror after horror, unalleviated by any of the splendours which other painters have been able to discover in war; for, significantly, Goya never illustrates an engagement, never shows us impressive masses of troops marching in column or deployed in the order of battle. His concern is exclusively with war as it affects the civilian population, with armies disintegrated into individual thieves and ravishers, tormentors and executioners—and occasionally, when the guerrilleros have won a skirmish, into individual victims tortured in their turn and savagely done to death by the avengers of their own earlier atrocities. All he shows us is war's disasters and squalors, without any of the glory or even picturesqueness.

In the two remaining series of etchings we pass from tragedy to satire and from historical fact to allegory and pictorial metaphor and pure fantasy. Twenty years separate the *Caprichos* from the *Disparates*, and the later collection is at once more sombre and more enigmatic than the earlier. Much of the satire of the *Caprichos* is merely Goya's sharper version of what may be called standard eighteenth-century humour. A plate such as *Hasta la Muerte*, showing the old hag before her mirror, coquettishly trying on a new head-dress, is just Rowlandson-with-a-difference. But in certain other etchings a stranger and more disquieting note is struck. Goya's handling of his material is such that standard eighteenth-century humour often undergoes a sea-change into something darker and queerer, something that goes below the anecdotal surface of life into what lies beneath—the unplumbed depths of original sin and original stupidity. And in the second half of the series the subject-matter reinforces the effect of the powerful and dramatically sinister treatment; for here the theme of almost all the plates is basely supernatural. We are in a world of demons, witches and familiars, half horrible, half comic, but wholly disquieting inasmuch as it reveals the sort of thing that goes on in the squalid catacombs of the human mind.

In the *Disparates* the satire is on the whole less direct than in the *Caprichos*, the allegories are more general and more mysterious. Consider, for example, the technically astonishing plate, which shows a large family of three generations perched like huddling birds along a huge dead branch that projects into the utter vacancy of a dark sky. Obviously, much more is meant than meets the eye. But what? The question is one upon which the commentators have spent a great deal of ingenuity—spent it, one may suspect, in vain. For the satire, it would seem, is not directed against this particular social evil or that political mistake, but rather against unregenerate human nature as such. It is a statement, in the form of an image, about life in general. Literature and the scriptures of all the great religions abound in such brief metaphorical verdicts on human destiny. Man turns the wheel of sorrow, burns in the fire of craving, travels through a vale of tears, leads a life that is no better than a tale told by an idiot signifying nothing.

Poor man, what art? A tennis ball of error,
A ship of glass tossed in a sea of terror:
Issuing in blood and sorrow from the womb,
Crawling in tears and mourning to the tomb.
How slippery are thy paths, how sure thy fall!
How art thou nothing, when thou art most of all!

And so on. Good, bad and indifferent, the quotations could be multiplied almost indefinitely. In the language of the plastic arts, Goya has added a score of memorable contributions to the stock of humanity's gnomic wisdom.

The *Disparate* of the dead branch is relatively easy to understand. So is the comment on Fear contained in the plate which shows soldiers running in terror from a gigantic cowled figure, spectral against a jet black sky. So is the etching of the ecstatically smiling woman riding a stallion that turns its head and, seizing her skirts between its teeth, tries to drag her from her seat. The allegorical use of the horse, as a symbol of the senses and the passions, and of the rational rider or charioteer who is at liberty to direct or be run away with, is at least as old as Plato.

But there are other plates in which the symbolism is less clear, the allegorical significance far from obvious. That horse on a tight-rope, for example, with a woman dancing on its back; the men who fly with artificial wings against a sky of inky menace; the priests and the elephant; the old man wandering among phantoms. What is the meaning of these things? And perhaps the answer to that question is that they have no meaning in any ordinary sense of the word; that they refer to strictly private events taking place on the obscurer levels of their creator's mind. For us who look at them, it may be that their real point and significance consist precisely in the fact that they image forth so vividly and yet, of necessity, so darkly and incomprehensibly, some at least of the unknown quantities that exist at the heart of every personality.

Goya once drew a picture of an ancient man tottering along under the burden of years, but with the accompanying caption, "I'm still learning." That old man was himself. To the end of a long life, he went on learning. As a very young man he paints like the feeble eclectics who were his masters. The first signs of power and freshness and originality appear in the cartoons for the tapestries, of which the earliest were executed when he was thirty. As a portraitist, however, he achieves nothing of outstanding interest until he is almost forty. But by that time he really knows what he's after, and during the second forty years of his life he moves steadily forward towards the consummate technical achievements, in oils, of the *Pinturas Negras*, and, in etching, of the *Desastres* and the *Disparates*. Goya's is a stylistic growth away from the restraint and into freedom, away from timidity and into expressive boldness.

From the technical point of view the most striking fact about almost all Goya's successful paintings and etchings is that they are composed in terms of one or more clearly delimited masses standing out from the background, often indeed silhouetted against the sky. When he attempts what may be called an 'all-over' composition, the essay is rarely successful. For he lacks almost completely the power which Rubens so conspicuously possessed—the power of filling the entire canvas with figures or details of landscape, and upon that *plenum* imposing a clear and yet exquisitely subtle three-dimensional order. The lack of this power is already conspicuous in the tapestry cartoons, of which the best are invariably those in which Goya does his composing in terms of silhouetted masses, and the worst those in which he attempts to organize a collection of figures distributed all over the canvas. And compare, from this point of view, the two paintings of the *Dos de Mayo*—the Mamelukes cutting down the crowd in the Puerta del Sol, and the firing squads at work in the suburbs, after dark. The first is an attempt to do what Rubens would have done with an almost excessive facility—to impose a formally beautiful and dramatically significant order upon a crowd of human and animal figures covering the greater part of the canvas. The attempt is not successful, and in spite of its power and the beauty of its component parts, the picture as a whole is less satisfying as a composition, and for that reason less moving as a story, than is the companion piece, in which Goya arranges his figures in a series of sharply delimited balancing groups, dramatically contrasted with one another and the background. In this picture the artist is speaking his native language, and he is therefore able to express what he wants to say with the maximum force and clarity. This is not the case with the picture of the Mamelukes. Here, the formal language is not truly his own, and consequently his eloquence lacks the moving power it possesses when he lets himself go in the genuine Goyescan idiom.

Fortunately, in the etchings, Goya is very seldom tempted to talk in anything else. Here he composes almost exclusively in terms of bold separate masses, silhouetted in luminous greys and whites against a darkness that ranges from stippled pepper-and-salt to intense black, or in blacks and heavily shaded greys against the whiteness of virgin paper. Sometimes there is only one mass, sometimes several, balanced and contrasted. Hardly ever does he make the, for him, almost fatal mistake of trying to organize his material in an all-over composition.

With the *Desastres* and the *Disparates* his mastery of

this, his predestined method of composition becomes, one might say, absolute. It is not, of course, the only method of composition. Indeed, the nature of this particular artistic idiom is such that there are probably certain things that can never be expressed in it—things which Rembrandt, for example, was able to say in his supremely beautiful and subtle illustrations to the Bible. But within the field that he chose to cultivate—that the idiosyncrasies of his temperament and the quality of his artistic sensibilities compelled him to choose—Goya remains incomparable.

THE DOUBLE CRISIS

THE human race is passing through a time of crisis, and that crisis exists, so to speak, on two levels—an upper level of political and economic crisis and a lower level of demographic and ecological crisis. That which is discussed at international conferences and in the newspapers is the upper-level crisis—the crisis whose immediate causes are the economic breakdown due to the War and the struggle for power between national groups possessing, or about to possess, the means of mass extermination. Of the low-level crisis, the crisis in population and world resources, hardly anything is heard in the press, on the radio or at the more important international conferences. The Big Threes and Big Fours do not deign to discuss it; leaving the matter to the subaltern and unauthoritative delegations to conferences on health or food, they devote their entire energies to the question of who shall bully whom. And yet the low-level crisis is at least as serious as the crisis in the political and economic field. Moreover, the problems on the upper level cannot be solved without reference to the problems that are shaping up in the cosmic and biological basement. If it is ignored, the low-level crisis is bound to exacerbate the crisis on the political and economic levels. At the same time, a concentration of attention and energy on power politics and power economics will make a solution of the low-level problems not merely difficult, but impossible. In what follows I propose to discuss certain aspects of the low-level crisis and to point out how the obscure happenings in the basement have affected and are likely to go on affecting the lives of private individuals, the policies of statesmen and the conduct of nations.

It has been fashionable for some time past to talk about "poverty in the midst of plenty." The phrase implies that the planet possesses abundant resources to feed, clothe, house and provide amenities for its existing population and for any immediately foreseeable increase in that population, and that the present miseries of the human race are due entirely to faulty methods of production and, above all, of distribution. Given currency reform, socialism, communism, unrestricted capitalism, distributism, or whatever the favourite remedy may be, humanity, like the prince and princess in the fairy stories, will be able to live happily ever after. Want and hunger will be transformed into abundance and the whole earth will become one vast Land of Cockayne.

Such are the miracles to be achieved by political and economic planning. But when we pass from these high-level considerations to a study of what is going on at the biological and ecological levels, our optimism is apt to seem a little premature, to say the least of it. Instead of poverty in the midst of plenty, we find that there is poverty in the midst of poverty. World resources are inadequate to world population. At the present time, our planet supports a little less than two and a quarter billions of human beings, and the area of food-producing land is in the neighbourhood of four billion acres. It has been calculated that two and a half acres of land are needed to provide a human being with a diet which nutritionists would regard as adequate. Thus, even if all the available productive land were good—and much of it is of very poor quality—the existing population could not be assured of an adequate diet. Actually, in order to guarantee an adequate diet for all of the world's two and a quarter billions of men, women and children, the present food supply would have to be doubled. But this cannot be accomplished overnight. In the words of Dr. Thomas Parran, the U.S. Surgeon-General, "the greatest possible increase in food production will not for decades be enough to meet the minimum adequate diet." And meanwhile world population is rising. It is rising at the rate of about two hundred millions every ten years. This means that, by the time the food supply is doubled, there will be, not two and a quarter billions of mouths to feed, but well over three billions. In spite of all that may have been achieved in the interval, malnutrition will be just as serious and just as widespread as it is today.

Moreover, while population goes up, the fertility of the soil declines. "Modern man," writes Ward Shepard in his *Food or Famine*, "has perfected two devices, either of which is capable of annihilating civilization. One is atomic war, the other is world soil-erosion. Of the two, soil-erosion is the more insidiously destructive. War disrupts or destroys the social environment, which is the matrix of civilization. Soil-erosion destroys the natural environment, which is its foundation." In other words, atomic war may destroy one particular civilization—the Western-Industrial variety, for example; soil-erosion, if unchecked, can put an end to the possibility of any civilization whatsoever.

The catalogue of man's crimes against his environment is long and dismal. In Africa the Sahara is advancing;

the habitable mountains and table-lands of the equator are rapidly eroding; the southern plains are over-grazed dust-bowls. Central America is in process of becoming a desert. Much of South America is being washed down unterraced mountain slopes into the sea. With every drought vast areas of Australia and the United States turn into wind-blown dust. In Asia it is the same lamentable story. As population goes up, the fertility of the ever more ruthlessly exploited land goes down. There is spreading and deepening human poverty in the midst of spreading and deepening natural poverty.

In certain respects the European picture is decidedly brighter. Thanks to sound agricultural practices and a climate that is without extremes, the farmers of Western Europe can produce good crops, and go on producing them, without, in the process, ruining their land. But however good these crops may be, they are insufficient to provide the present population of the territory with its minimum food requirements. In relation to the local resources Western Europe is overpopulated. In England, Belgium, Holland, Italy and the Western zones of Germany, there is less than one acre of food-producing land for each inhabitant. And even where the density of population is lower than in these countries the productive land available is still insufficient to provide a full diet (to say nothing of the necessary timber and fibres) for the local inhabitants. According to some competent authorities, even Russia is overpopulated. The short northern summer severely limits the size of the crops, and the long northern winter severely limits the number of animals that can be kept alive on stored-up fodder. And over the greater part of the country precipitation is low and irregular. In these circumstances even a low population density may be excessive. And the birth-rate is high, modern hygiene and medicine are prolonging the expectation of life, numbers are rapidly increasing. But meanwhile new methods of arctic agriculture have been devised; ambitious schemes of irrigating Central Asia are under study; and, having abolished the laws of 'reactionary genetics,' Lysenko promises a revolution in plant-breeding. Will the tundras, the deserts and ideologically correct science be able to feed and clothe the two hundred and fifty millions who will inhabit the U.S.S.R. in 1970? Let us hope so; for the alternative is a crusade for more *lebensraum*.

Since 1800 Western Europe has more than trebled its population. This huge increase was made possible by elementary hygiene and the exploitation of the virgin territories of the New World. Today hygiene and medicine are keeping more Europeans alive; but the New World has a large and rapidly increasing population of its own and, after more than a century of abuse, not a little of its soil has lost or is in process of losing its fertility. In a good year there is still a very large exportable surplus. But not every season is a good season. During the lean years of the thirties, the United States had very little to sell abroad. And here we may remark that the success of the Marshall Plan and, indeed, the whole outcome of the Cold War depend, among other things, on the weather. Consider, for example, this by no means impossible contingency: for three years in succession Russia has bumper wheat crops, while the harvests of Western Europe, North America, Australia and the Argentine are ruined by drought or excessive rains. In these circumstances, who will control the world —the people with the atomic bombs, or the people with bread? Obviously, the people with bread.

Up to the present, Western Europe has contrived to pay for the food imported from the New World by selling manufactured articles and technical services. With the industrialization of the New World, these are becoming less and less acceptable. Europe will find it increasingly difficult to pay for supplies which, as the population pressure on the New World's eroded soils increases, are bound to diminish. And this will happen at a time when Asia, newly industrialized and overcrowded as never before, will be desperately competing for whatever surpluses of food the New World can still make available to the Old.

Food is a renewable commodity. If the soil is not abused, this year's harvest will be succeeded next year by another harvest no less bountiful. But the vein of tin or copper, which was the source of this year's supply of ore, will not be renewed in years to come. When the lode has been worked out, the miner must move on to another deposit of the mineral. And if he can find no other deposits? *Après moi le déluge*. Industrialism is the systematic exploitation of wasting assets. In all too many cases, the thing we call progress is merely an acceleration in the rate of that exploitation. Such prosperity as we have known up to the present is the consequence of rapidly spending the planet's irreplaceable capital.

How long can the accelerating dissipation of capital go on? How soon will the wasting assets of the world be exhausted? We do not know. All that is certain is that the supplies of many hitherto essential commodities are limited and that, in many places, very rich and easily available deposits of those commodities have been, or are in process of being, worked out. And this is happening at a time when a rising population with steadily improving methods of production is calling for ever-increasing quantities of consumer goods—in other words, is making ever heavier demands on the limited reserves of our planetary capital.

Up to this point, I have dealt with world population as a single undifferentiated whole. The problem thus posed is that of increasing pressure upon diminishing resources. But this basic problem of our time is deepened and complicated by the fact that rates of increase are not uniform throughout the world's population. Differential birth-rates as between the various peoples of the earth, and as between classes within a people, are rapidly engendering a host of new problems.

In Western Europe and North America, the over-all birth-rate has sharply declined in the course of the last fifty or sixty years. Because of the lowered death-rate and the relatively large numbers of persons within the reproductive age-groups, this decline in the birth-rate has not yet manifested itself in a net decline of population. But the onset of such a decline is close at hand. For example, by 1970 the population of France and Great Britain will have declined by about four millions apiece, and the number of persons over sixty-five will be approximately equal to the number of those under fifteen. Similar declines are due, at a slightly later date, in the other countries of Western Europe and in the New World (except South America). Meanwhile, in spite of much higher death-rates, the population of Eastern Europe and of Asia is destined to go on increasing. By the end of the present century, Asia alone will have a population of about two billions. And in 1970, when Western Europe will have some nine million fewer inhabitants than it possesses today, Russia will have gained upwards of fifty millions.

Within any nation whose birth-rate is declining, there is a tendency for the decline to be most rapid among the most accomplished and gifted members of the population, least rapid among those whose hereditary and educational endowment is the lowest. The higher the Intelligence Quotient and the level of education, the smaller the family; and vice versa. The future population of Western Europe and North America will be constituted, in the main, by the descendants of the least intelligent persons now living in those areas. Among the lower animals, biological degeneration, involving the heritable qualities of whole populations, is a slow and gradual process. But human beings differ from other animals in possessing self-consciousness and a measure of free-will, and in being the inhabitants of a man-made universe within the greater natural order. Reacting to what goes on in this man-made universe, they use their free-will to modify their basic patterns of animal behaviour. And when the nature of the human universe is such as to discourage the more sensitive, intelligent and prudent individuals from reproducing their kind, the deterioration of entire societies comes about with an almost explosive rapidity. Thus an eminent English authority, Sir Cyril Burt, foresees that by the end of the present century, there will be, in Great Britain, half as many children of scholarship ability as there are at present, and twice as many defectives; while the average intelligence of the population as a whole will have declined by five IQ points. And the case of Britain is not unique. Throughout Western Europe, and, a little later, in North America, the decline in numbers is destined to be accompanied by a rapid deterioration in the quality of the population.

We have now to consider the ways in which these untoward biological happenings have affected, or are likely in the future to affect, our behaviour on the levels of domestic and international politics.

The nature of the low-level crisis is such that it must necessarily take a very long time to remove its underlying causes. The best we can do is to palliate the more dangerous symptoms and to draw up plans for a genuinely etiological treatment.

Differential birth-rates within any national community lead, as we have seen, to a qualitative deterioration of the population as a whole. The effects of such a deterioration have not yet made themselves felt, and it is hard to foresee in detail what they will be. We must be content merely to pose a question. Is it possible for democratic institutions to flourish in a community in which the incidence of outstanding ability is falling, while that of mental defect is rising? Fifty years from now our grandchildren will know the answer. In the interval it will be necessary to develop new types of training designed to get the best out of worsening human material and to find means for inducing the congenitally gifted to reproduce their kind.

Where the birth-rate of an entire nation declines sharply, while that of its neighbours remains high, we must expect, in the world as it is now constituted, a more or less serious threat to peace. Regardless of what faiths may currently be professed, the real and effective religion of twentieth-century man is nationalistic idolatry. Nominally we may be Christians or Buddhists or Hindus or Moslems or Jews; but in actual fact we worship, not one God, but fifty or sixty godlets, each of whom is, by definition, the enemy, actual or potential, of all the rest. In every country where there is no established church, the only religion taught in the public schools is some local variant of Shintoism—a saluting of flags, a cult of the State and, very often, of the men who control its machinery, a glorification of the national prowess, as set forth in the official history books. Entities which are the accidental and transient products of history are treated as though they were divine, as though they embodied principles of eternal and universal validity. From childhood the citizen is taught that his highest duty is to work for the greater glory of the local idol. But since this glory is expressed mainly in terms of political and military power, it follows that no individual can do his nationalistic duty without inflicting harm on some at least of his fellow men. In the context of nationalistic idolatry, any shift in the balance of power constitutes a temptation to wage war, aggressive on the part of those nations which are becoming stronger, defensive or preventive on the part of those whose situation is changing for the worse. Such a shift will take place wherever the birth-rates of two equally industrialized nations change in such a way that one has an increasing and predominantly youthful population, while the other has a population that is growing smaller, older and perhaps also less intelligent.

Populations increase and decrease relatively not only to one another, but also to natural resources. In most parts of the world, as we have seen, the relation between population and resources is already unfavourable and will probably become even more unfavourable in the future. This growing poverty in the midst of growing poverty constitutes a permanent menace to peace. And not only to peace, but also to democratic institutions and personal liberty. For overpopulation is not compatible with freedom. An unfavourable relationship between numbers and resources tends to make the earning of a living almost intolerably difficult. Labour is more abundant than goods, and the individual is compelled to work long hours for little pay. No surplus of accumulated purchasing power stands between him and the tyrannies of unfriendly nature or of the equally unfriendly wielders of political and economic power. Democracy is, among other things, the ability to say No to the boss. But a man cannot say No to the boss, unless he is sure of being able to eat when the boss's favour has been withdrawn. And he cannot be certain of his next meal unless he owns the means of producing enough wealth for his family to live on, or has been able to accumulate a surplus out of past wages, or has a chance of moving away to virgin territories, where he can make a fresh start. In an overcrowded country, very few people own enough to make them financially independent; very few are in a position to accumulate purchasing power; and there is no free land. Moreover, in any country where population presses hard upon natural resources, the general economic situation is apt to be so precarious that government control of capital and labour, production and consumption, becomes inevitable. It is no accident that the twentieth century should be the century of highly centralized governments and totalitarian dictatorships; it had to be so for the simple reason that the twentieth century is the century of planetary overcrowding. It is childish to imagine that we can "plant democratic institutions" in India, or China, or "teach the Germans to take their place among the democratic nations of the world." So long as the relationship between population and natural resources remains as hopelessly unfavourable as it now is throughout Asia and in the greater part of Europe, above all in defeated Germany, it will be for all practical purposes impossible for democratic institutions to take root and develop. Wherever Malthus's nightmare has come true, political institutions tend inevitably towards totalitarianism. In Western Europe, where the tradition of democracy is still strong, the new totalitarianism will be for some time benevolent and humane. It remains to be seen how long it will be before their almost absolute power corrupts the politicians who wield it.

In the political field, the greatest enemy to liberty is war. That is why, from time immemorial, all tyrants have been so fond of war, or at least of the preparation for war. Universal military conscription puts every individual at the mercy of the central government. An aggressive foreign policy evokes reactions in kind, and these reactions are then used as an excuse for more militarism and a further curtailment of civil and personal liberties. Dictators can always consolidate their tyranny by an appeal to patriotism. Meanwhile, the danger of war is made a pretext for a policy, not of reducing, but actually increasing the birth-rate—a policy which was vigorously pursued by Hitler and Mussolini and is being even more vigorously pursued today by the rulers of Soviet Russia.

More babies mean more cannon fodder, more colonists for conquered territories, and also more misery, more need for centralized 'planning' and more power for the political bosses, less liberty for the masses. Overcrowding and militarism are the guarantees of dictatorship.

In our days war on any considerable scale can be waged only by a highly industrialized nation. There can be no successful aggression without the copious and complicated armaments which are the modern means of aggression. Lacking these means, the people of an over-populated country are confronted with only two alternatives. They can either stop breeding, and so reduce the population. Or else they can go on breeding until famine, disease, political unrest and civil war combine to raise the death-rate to the point where a decreased population can re-establish a favourable relationship with natural resources. But some overpopulated countries are also industrialized; and for these there is a third alternative: to enslave or exterminate their neighbours, and so acquire more land, food, raw materials and markets.

It should be added that, though they cannot themselves wage large-scale war, industrially weak nations can provoke and assist in the waging of war by industrially powerful nations. An unfavourable relationship between numbers and resources is experienced, by the less fortunate citizens of an overpopulated nation, as chronic hunger, low wages, long hours, lack of freedom and opportunity. The resulting discontent is apt to be expressed in political unrest and revolt against constituted authority. At the present time all political unrest, whatever its cause, tends to be rationalized in terms of Communist theory and organized in terms of Communist power politics. But at this moment of history Communism is, among other things, the instrument of Russian nationalism, and Russia is an industrialized country, capable of waging large-scale war and committed in advance to a permanent crusade against the West.

Let us consider a concrete example. Throughout Asia a misery, whose basic cause is the unfavourable relation between numbers and resources, finds its expression in political unrest. Canalized by professional Communists, this unrest may be expected to result in the setting up of governments which will do everything in their power to aid Russia and to thwart the plans of the Western Powers. Merely by withholding essential raw materials, a communist Asia could delay or even completely prevent European recovery. The West would then find itself confronted by the alternatives of surrender or preventive war. Thus we see that the overpopulation even of industrially feeble nations may constitute a grave threat to world peace.

In the world as we know it nation A will collaborate whole-heartedly with nation B only when both are menaced by C. During a war that is being waged to preserve their national sovereignty, a group of allies will consent to sacrifice a part of that sovereignty for the sake of victory. But as soon as victory has been achieved, the allied nations return to their normal condition of more or less hostile symbiosis, ready, however, to collaborate again, either with the same or with some other partners, against the same or another enemy.

On the international level, union here is always the product of disunion somewhere else; there is no unrestricted mutual aid except against a third party. Hence the old despairing jest to the effect that those who desire peace on earth should pray for an invasion from Mars. But, fortunately in one respect, unfortunately in another, we do not have to wait for an attack across interplanetary space. Man is his own Martian, at war against himself. Overbreeding and extractive agriculture are his weapons and, though he may not know it, his war aims are the ravaging of his planet, the destruction of his civilization and the degradation of his species.

That the nations have not yet united against this common enemy within their own ranks is due partly to the distracting influence of nationalistic idolatry, partly to ignorance, and partly to men's habit of thinking about the problem in wholly inappropriate terms. Time, energy and money that could be better spent are everywhere devoted to power politics and preparations for war. And meanwhile, throughout the more fortunate regions of the earth, most persons are still unaware of the fact that the general condition of mankind is one of poverty in the midst of growing poverty; and in the less fortunate regions, where the harsh facts are inescapable, there is a tendency to believe that the remedy for such poverty is a violent and radical change of government. The inhabitants of countries, in which there is an unfavourable relationship between numbers and resources, can easily be persuaded that the causes of their misery are political and that, as soon as their present rulers are replaced by others trained in Moscow, all will be well. But one-party government is no cure for overpopulation, and the collectivization of agriculture will not increase the area of productive land.

It has been fashionable for a long time past to maintain that the reformer's primary concern is with questions of ownership and distribution. And, in effect, distribution is often inefficient and unfair, and there can be no moral or utilitarian justification for that outright and irresponsible ownership of land which permits a man to withhold or destroy at his pleasure the natural resources upon which the life of a whole society depends.

We need a new system of money that will deliver us from servitude to the banks and permit people to buy what they are able to produce; and we need a new system of ownership that will check the tendency towards monopoly in land and make it impossible for individuals to lay waste the planetary resources which belong to all mankind. But changes in social and economic organization are not enough, of themselves, to solve our problem. Production is inadequate to present population, and population, over large areas, is rapidly rising. A change in the laws governing the ownership of land will not change its quantity or quality. The equitable distribution of too little may satisfy men's desire for justice; it will not stay their hunger. In a world where population is growing at the rate of about fifty-six thousand a day, and where erosion is daily ruining an equal or perhaps greater number of productive acres, our primary concern must be with reducing numbers and producing more food with less damage to the soil.

Sooner or later mankind will be forced by the pressure of circumstances to take concerted action against its own destructive and suicidal tendencies. The longer such action is postponed, the worse it will be for all concerned. To delay is to risk the spread and intensification of misery, to invite revolution, war and tyranny. But if we start at once to resolve the low-level crisis, there is at least a chance that we may escape the most disastrous consequences of nationalistic idolatry and power politics.

The history of the League of Nations and of the United Nations Organization proves conclusively that, on the basis of nationalistic idolatry and power politics, there cannot possibly be co-operation between all the world's sovereign states; there can only be co-operation of one group against another group. Overpopulation and erosion constitute a Martian invasion of the planet. Against this invasion the alliance can be world-wide and the fight can be waged without war. This is the first reason why the low-level crisis should take its place at the top of the agenda of every international conference.

Here is another reason. There is nobody who does not wish to have enough to eat. In the face of this universal agreement any government which, for merely political or ideological reasons, refuses to join the crusade against the Martian in our midst is likely to become exceedingly unpopular.

A third good reason is to be found in the fact that this crusade is mainly a technological affair. Differences of opinion over technological problems rarely result in bloodshed; differences of opinion over political and ideological problems have been the cause of uncounted murders, feuds, wars and revolutions. Here violence is in direct proportion to ignorance. About technological problems we either know enough already, or if we do not, we know how to set about acquiring the necessary knowledge. But where politics and ideologies are concerned the case is very different. For example, nobody knows enough to be able to decide whether a certain theory of history is true or false or meaningless. And nobody knows enough to be able to say which among all the possible alternatives is the form of government best suited to human societies. In regard to the theory of history it seems very unlikely that the necessary knowledge will ever be accumulated. And in regard to any given form of government, knowledge can come only with the passage of time. Future events in the material universe can, to some extent, be foreseen; but our ability to predict psychological events is practically non-existent. How will our children and grandchildren react to forms of organizations which, to ourselves, seem the last word in beneficent efficiency? Will they like what we like, or will they detest it? Will an arrangement which works well enough for us, work equally well for them? We do not and we cannot know. That is why we must never take the practical application of a principle as seriously as the principle which is being applied. Thus, we may take very seriously the principle that the State exists in order to make possible the development of individuals as free and responsible persons. But we must not take too seriously any particular plan for applying that principle in political and economic practice. The mere passage of time may demonstrate the unsoundness of any particular application of first principles. To treat political expedients as though they were sacred and inviolable is to commit an idolatry that can only result in totalitarian coercion. Thus, in our ignorance, we do not know whether the Webbs were right in advocating centralized planning as the best means to the desired end, or whether Belloc was right in warning us against the evils of the Servile State. Time alone will show; and when it begins to show, we must be ready, in the name of our principles, to modify the policy which, in our ignorance, we once regarded as the most effective application of those principles. Unfortunately there are very many persons to whom the admission of ignorance is intolerable. Laying claim to certainty in spheres where certainty is impossible, to infallibility concerning matters where even a Pope admits that he can err, they rationalize faith, passion and self-interest into a simulacrum of knowledge. Hence the wars, the revolutions, the tyrannies, the wholesale enslavement of political heretics. A pseudo-knowledge compounded of faith, passion and self-interest cannot convince doubters or the exponents of another system of pseudo-knowledge, except by force. Real knowledge is based upon observation and experiment; and those who possess such knowledge are always able to appeal to facts and the tested rules of scientific procedure. In the technological sphere there can be unforced agreement and persuasion without resort to threats or open violence. We should therefore give approval to any international project which may distract the attention of the world's rulers from the insoluble and war-provoking problems of power politics in order to focus it upon problems which, being technological, admit of some solution and do not necessarily commit all those concerned to fratricide and self-destruction. And in the case of a project which cannot be delayed except at grave risk to the entire human species, our approval should be whole-hearted and enthusiastic.

That the Russians have been 'winning the peace' is due, at least in part, to the fact that they profess and teach, as absolutely true, a clear-cut philosophy of man and nature. This philosophy permits them to predict the future and to affirm (with a confidence which, though unjustified and baseless, is none the less deeply impressive) that, if a certain kind of political and economic revolution is made, general well-being will inevitably follow. In the West we neither impose, nor have we voluntarily accepted, any coherent conception of the world; we lay no claims to understand History from the inside; we do not profess to know in advance what is going to happen fifty or a hundred years from now; and when we are called upon to frame world policies, we find it easier, because of our lack of a philosophy, to be *against* the Russians than to be *for* anything which the great masses of suffering humanity are likely to find either plausible or attractive. The Western refusal to assert an infallibility or to impose an orthodoxy is something of which we need not be ashamed. Less creditable, however, is the fact that we have failed to develop a generally acceptable philosophy for ourselves and for those whom we would like to draw to our side; and still more discreditable is our failure to formulate any policy sensible and beneficent enough to seem more attractive than the policies of Communism. The nearest approach to such a positive policy was the Marshall Plan. But the Marshall Plan has now (1949) been overlaid by military alliance, and military alliances seem attractive only to those immediately involved and (in view of the past history of military alliances) not wildly attractive even to them.

The positive, realistic and universally attractive policy of which the Western Powers are so desperately in need can easily be found. It is a policy aimed at palliating the effects and removing the causes of that low-level crisis through which the entire human species is passing. If the Russians are willing to co-operate in the framing and carrying out of this policy, so much the better. If they refuse and the Cold War is to persist, this policy can be made into a powerful diplomatic and propagandist weapon in the hands of the democracies. Its adoption will not, of course, guarantee peace in our time; but it may perhaps decrease the probabilities of war in the immediate and, still more, in the remoter future. Let us consider in detail the lines along which our policy should be framed.

The world's economic and political crisis has its origin, at least in part, in the underlying demographical crisis. In most countries the relationship between numbers and resources is unfavourable. Nature has her own methods for re-establishing a favourable balance; but, applied to human beings living under twentieth-century conditions, such methods involve not merely intense and widespread misery, but also the gravest threat to civilization. Stated in its most general terms, the problem is to reconcile biological facts with human values.

Our first task is to create a general awareness of the danger. At every opportunity we must insist upon the fact that man is his own Martian, that the invasion of the planet is already under way, and that fresh cohorts are constantly arriving to swell the ranks simultaneously of the enemy and of his victims. At the same time we have to proclaim no less insistently that the miseries resulting from this Martian invasion cannot be removed by any revolution, however radical. Overpopulation and erosion do their destructive work on a plane which is not that of politics. A concerted attempt to cope with events on the demographical and agricultural plane may indirectly exercise a salutary effect upon international politics. But an attempt to impose one kind of political system upon all the peoples of the earth will do nothing whatever to resolve the low-level crisis, but on the contrary will prevent men from doing anything about it and thereby increase the sum and intensity of preventable misery. The low-level crisis can be resolved in only two ways—by controlling world population and by increasing food production, while restoring and preserving the earth's fertility.

Man cannot live by bread alone; but still less can he live exclusively by idealism. To talk about the Rights of Man and the Four Freedoms in connection, for example, with India is merely a cruel joke. In a country where two-thirds of the people succumb to the consequences of malnutrition before they reach the age of thirty, but where, none the less, the population increases by fifty millions every decade, most men possess neither rights nor any kind of freedom. The 'giant misery of the world' is only aggravated by mass violence and cannot be mitigated by inspirational twaddle. Misery will yield only to an intelligent attack upon the causes of misery.

It is, of course, a great deal easier to talk about a world population policy than it is to get such a policy accepted by the various national governments; and it will be easier to get the policy accepted than to get it implemented. Moreover, even if it should, by some miracle, come to be accepted and implemented immediately, the beneficent results could not, in the nature of things, be apparent for several generations. Let us elaborate a little on this depressing theme.

So long as idolatrous nationalism remains the effective religion of mankind, and so long as it is taken for granted that war is right, proper and inevitable, no government of a country with a high birth-rate will pledge itself to the reduction of that rate; and no government of a country with a low birth-rate will forgo in advance the privilege of trying to increase that rate with a view to increasing the size of its armed forces.

Assuming now, for the sake of argument, that, in spite of nationalism and militarism, a world population policy should be agreed upon, how easy would it be to get that policy implemented? The answer is that, in the countries where its immediate implementation would be most desirable, it would be exceedingly difficult, indeed almost impossible, to do so. For a variety of reasons, material and psychological, birth-control cannot be practised by persons whose standard of living falls below a level which, for the great majority of Asiatics and even of Eastern Europeans, is unattainably high. To obtain any conscious or deliberate reduction of the high birth-rates prevailing in the East would be a task requiring many years of education and technological advance.

Finally, even if a substantial cut in the present high birth-rates of the world were to be agreed upon and successfully implemented tomorrow, the number of persons in the reproductive age-groups is at present so large that, despite the reduced birth-rate, over-all population would continue to increase until at least the end of the present century. In the most favourable circumstances we can reasonably imagine, world population is bound to rise to at least three billions before it starts to decline. This means that, whatever happens, the next half-century will be a time of the gravest political and economic danger. If a world population policy should be agreed upon and implemented in the near future, this danger may be expected to grow less acute after about the year 2000. If no such policy is adopted, the crisis is likely, unless something startlingly good or something startlingly bad should happen in the interval, to persist for many years thereafter. So far as we can now judge, the human situation is likely to be more than ordinarily difficult and precarious for at least two generations, and perhaps for much longer. The sooner we can get a reasonable population policy adopted and implemented, the shorter will be the period of special danger through which, it would seem, mankind must inevitably pass.

Here a brief parenthesis is in order. In this matter of population we are on the horns of a dilemma. For what is good for us in one way, is bad in another; and what is bad in one way, in another is good. Biologically and historically speaking, the large family is more normal than the small. A woman who has borne five or six children is 'nearer to nature' than one who has artificially restricted the number to one or two. In countries where the birth-rate is sharply declining, there has been, during the last forty years, a marked increase in the incidence of neurosis and even of insanity. In part this increase is attributable to the industrialization and urbanization with which, in modern times, a falling birth-rate has always been associated; in part, to the fact that birth-control has created patterns of sexual and familial life which are in some way profoundly unsatisfactory to adults and children alike. Wherever biologically normal behaviour has been sacrificed to modern civilization, we tend to become maladjusted and unbalanced. But wherever biologically normal behaviour patterns have not been sacrificed to modern civilization, we find ourselves growing hungrier, less free and in acuter danger of being involved in war and revolution. On which of these two horns shall we choose to be impaled? To my mind, the first is the lesser evil. Overpopulation, with its accompaniments of extractive agriculture, tyranny and mass murder, can cause irreparable disasters. Of the bad psychological consequences of birth-control some perhaps may yield to appropriate medication, others may be prevented, by appropriate social arrangements, from ever arising. Departure from biologically normal behaviour is always dangerous; but the dangers involved in birth-control are not so great as those which arise when individuals retain their natural breeding habits in a world where hygiene, insecticides, antibiotics and false teeth have radically changed their natural dying habits. If we interfere with the forces that bring death, we must also interfere with those that bring life. Otherwise we shall have overpopulation, an unfavourable relationship between man and his environment, wholesale destruction of planetary resources, hunger, revolution, war and wholesale extermination. Given sewage systems, aureomycin and plastic dentures, contraception becomes a necessity and the adoption of a world population policy a matter of the most urgent importance. Unfortunately, as we have seen, a world population policy cannot be expected to show results for many years to come. But while we are waiting for it to take effect we can set to work immediately on the task of checking erosion, preserving the fertility of the soil and increasing the production of food.

At the present time most nations are quite incapable of undertaking this task single-handed. They live from hand to mouth; and the mouth is for ever growing larger, the hand, as it desperately tries to extract more food from a limited area of exhausted soil, becomes increasingly destructive. For these nations there is no margin of time, or land, or resources. Everything, and more than everything, that their territory can produce has to be used up now. Future fertility must be sacrificed to present hunger. In a country where population presses heavily upon resources self-preservation results in self-destruction.

If the Western Powers had a positive instead of a mainly negative international policy, they would come forward with a plan to check this rake's progress towards human and planetary bankruptcy. Or rather they would come forward with several plans. First, a plan to repair the damage already done to the earth's cultivated lands; second, a plan to replace destructive methods of farming and forestry by methods more in harmony with the laws of nature; and, third, a plan to discover and develop new sources of supply.

The cost of carrying out the first two plans would be high—though certainly no higher than the cost of preparing to win the Third World War and crush the First World Revolution. It would be high because, in order to give eroded land a chance to recover its fertility, it would be necessary for a period of years to relieve the pressure imposed upon it by an excessive population. In other words, it would be necessary to provide overcrowded countries with an amount of food equal to the difference between what they might have extracted from the soil by ruinous exploitation and what, under the plan, they are able to extract, while checking erosion and preparing the shift to better agricultural methods. It would also be necessary to subsidize the migration to safer areas of those persons now living on specially vulnerable watersheds. Additional funds would have to be found for supplying experts to technologically backward countries, for training nationals of those countries in sound agriculture and the theory and practice of conservation, and for undertaking a world-wide survey of soils, climates and natural resources.

The third plan would be in the nature of a vast international project for research and experimentation. To men of science and technicians recruited from every part of the world would be assigned the task of discovering new ways, not of murdering their fellows, but of feeding and clothing them. Let us consider a few of the more obvious possibilities that will have to be explored.

Large areas of the earth's surface are uninhabited because, under present conditions, they are uninhabitable. But in some of these areas the expenditure of much capital and hard work might render the land productive. At present the development of deserts, tundras and tropical forests is prohibitively costly; but as population rises and the demand for food and fibres yet further outstrips supply, what is now uneconomic may come to be a 'business proposition.' It will be the business of our hypothetical board of experts to decide which areas are to be developed, when the development shall take place, and at what expenditure of international funds.

It is desirable that the world's total food supply should be increased, and increased in any way whatsoever. But let us always remember that, from a political point of view, the most satisfactory kind of increase is one which does not involve a natural monopoly by specially favoured nations. In the context of nationalism, a natural monopoly in food surpluses can become an instrument by means of which one nation, or group of nations, may coerce other nations less fortunate than themselves. Ideally, the world's food supply should be increased in such a way that the increase shall not strengthen existing natural monopolies, or create new ones, but shall permit every nation to live on supplies grown on its own land or coming from sources equally available to all mankind. Under existing circumstances, international trade is as much of a curse as a blessing. It will become an unmitigated blessing only when nationalistic idolatry shall have ceased to be the effective religion of mankind.

Meanwhile we should do everything in our power to foster national, or at least regional, self-sufficiency in the prime necessities of existence. A step in this direction would be taken if we could develop means for getting more food from the sea. At the present time most of the seas in the neighbourhood of densely populated areas are being over-fished. More effort has to be put forth in order to obtain a diminishing harvest of fish—and this at a time when we need more food to satisfy the growing population. Can the oceans be made to yield new sources of supply? Can sea-weeds be processed into fodder and manure? What about plankton? What about the enclosure and fertilizing of landlocked bays and inlets?

But some countries have no access to the sea. Even salt water is a natural monopoly. Our international board of researchers must consider yet other ways of achieving regional self-sufficiency. What about the transformation of poor land into productive fish-ponds? What about the cultivation of fresh-water algae for fodder? What about the conversion of sawdust and vegetable wastes into sugar solutions for the cultivation of edible yeasts? And the bacteria with their tremendous capacity for bringing about chemical transformations—can any of these be domesticated and set to work producing food for man?

Natural monopolies in minerals are perhaps even more dangerous, politically speaking, than natural monopolies in food surpluses. When located in the territory of a strong nation with a culture orientated towards aggressive enterprise, deposits of coal, petroleum and the metals necessary to heavy industry are a standing temptation to imperialist expansion. When located in the territory of a weak nation, they are a standing invitation to aggression from abroad. Research should be systematically directed to the development of universally available surrogates for the present sources of power and industrial production—for example, wind-power and sun-power, in combination with an efficient storage battery, as a supplement and partial substitute for power derived from coal and petroleum; glass, plastics, light metals derived from clay and sea-water as partial substitutes for the capriciously distributed minerals upon which industry at present depends. By these means we might perhaps succeed in breaking the natural monopolies which are so politically dangerous; and at the same time we should be doing something to shift our industrial civilization from its precarious basis in the exploitation of rapidly wasting assets to a more secure, a more nearly permanent foundation.

We now come to the henceforth inescapable fact of nuclear fission. For us the question is simple: how can nuclear fission help us in resolving the low-level crisis? In the immediate future its greatest contribution will probably be made in the field of genetics. By exposing seeds to the gamma rays emanating from an atomic pile, we can produce large numbers of unprecedented mutations. The overwhelming majority of these mutations will be harmful; but a few may result in varieties not merely viable, but even economically useful—varieties yielding more of this or that food element, varieties capable of maturing under climatic conditions which would be fatal to the parent strain, varieties resistant to certain diseases and parasites, and so forth.

Theoretically and ideally, nuclear fission should provide cheap power for developing territories too arid, or too cold, or too rugged, or too remote from the conventional sources of power to be worth exploiting under present conditions. In practice, however, atomic power is likely to remain for some time to come a very expensive luxury. Twenty years from now it may be that the dream of almost costless power will have been realized. It will be none too soon; for twenty years from now the planet will have to support a population greater by four hundred millions than its population today. And meanwhile every lunatic in a position of power, every fanatic, every idealist, every patriot will be under chronic temptation to use the new source of energy for political purposes, in a war of aggression, or prevention, or defence. To purchase advantages which, in the short and middle run, are not likely to be very great, we must run risks so enormous as to be incommensurable with a conceivable gain. One is reminded of Pascal's wager. We are betting on a strictly finite good against the far from remote possibility of an evil that, for practical purposes, may be regarded as infinite.

In a world where nationalism is axiomatic and where the differences between politico-religious ideologies are as irreconcilable as they were in the days of the Crusades, an international project for the relief of hunger and the conservation of our planetary resources seems to offer the best and perhaps the only hope for peace and international co-operation. At this point, the sponsors of world federation will object that our project cannot be carried out except by a world government. Political union, they will say, must come first; economic and technological collaboration will then follow as a matter of course. But at the present time, unfortunately, the governments of most nations do not want union. Or, to be more accurate, they want union, but do not want the means to union. For the means to political union entail immediate sacrifices which it would not be pleasant to make. For example, in a politically federated Europe many local industries, which have been fostered and protected by national tariffs, would prove to be redundant and would either have to be suppressed by government fiat, or would find themselves ruined by the competition of industries more efficiently managed or more favourably situated in relation to raw materials and markets. The suppression of redundant industries would cause much hardship among owners, managers and workers alike. And this is only one of the costs of political union. Enormous advantages in the long run can be secured only by a number of rather painful sacrifices in the short run. Political union can be imposed by force, under a military dictatorship; or under the pressure of circumstances. During periods of 'normalcy' the political union of sovereign, democratic states is much harder to achieve. Men and women will not vote for a policy which entails the immediate loss of their jobs and a disturbing change in their habits. As a general rule, it is only in times of crisis that people are willing to make sacrifices now for the sake of a good in the future. All the higher religions are, among other things, devices for convincing human beings that their every moment is a moment of crisis, involving matters of spiritual life and death, and that therefore it is reasonable as well as right to make certain sacrifices. On quite another level every moment in the life of human beings on an overcrowded and eroding planet is also a moment of crisis. To explain the nature of man's Martian aggression against himself and to convince the masses of the necessity of concerted action against the invasion should not be too difficult, all the more so as the immediate sacrifices involved will not be excessive and the advantages to be expected in the long and middle run are so concrete, evident and appealing. Once established, this primarily technological alliance against the Martian forces of overpopulation and erosion can be expected to develop into a political and economic collaboration which, in its turn, may prove to be the precursor of genuine world federation under a single authority. If, in the meantime, federation can be achieved by purely political means, so much the better. It does not matter which comes first, the political chicken or the technological egg. What is important is that, in some way or other, we should get both, and get them with the least possible delay.

And meanwhile we may hope that the habit of collaboration upon a project that so obviously concerns the whole of mankind may do something to undermine, among rulers as well as ruled, that nationalistic idolatry which is the prime political cause of all our high-level crises. Nationalism is an artificial thing, but an artificial thing which has its roots in the individual's quasi-instinctive attachment to the environment of his childhood—to a place, to a dietary, to a set of habits, customs and conventions, to a language and the people who speak that language. Such local patriotism is found on the sub-human level. Birds, for example, will fight for their territory; the sentries at the entrance to a hive will attack and kill any bee belonging to another swarm. The first is an example of rugged individualism—"an Englishman's home is his castle"; the second, of collective xenophobia—"every Western visitor is a class-enemy of the U.S.S.R." Among human beings, tribal sentiment is the nearest approach to a natural and unsophisticated expression of the quasi-instinct of local patriotism. Tribes have now given place to nations; and this has happened because rulers found that it was possible, by means of suitable education and propaganda, to transfer the quasi-instinctive sentiment of tribalism from its natural object to a new, artificial object—the nation. The home place and the home people can be touched, seen, directly experienced. It is therefore possible for a man to love them in an almost physiological way. The nation is too large to be an object of immediate acquaintance and, for any given individual within the nation, is hardly more than an abstraction. But the abstraction can be symbolically represented by an object (the flag), by a person (the

King, the Leader), by a tune and a form of words (the Star-spangled Banner, the Internationale). These symbolic representations can be immediately experienced and loved, not merely with the head, but also with the heart, the yearning bowels. It is by means of symbols that men and women have been educated out of tribal patriotism and into nationalistic idolatry. And symbols, no doubt, will be used when the moment comes to educate them out of nationalistic idolatry and into world-patriotism. In Western Europe it took several centuries for capitalistic thought-patterns to replace the thought-patterns of feudal society. How many years will pass before humanity at large can be made to forget the nationalistic axioms on which so much of its current thinking and feeling is based and to accept in their place the axioms of a non-nationalistic system? Anyone who would hazard a guess must take into account two facts: first, that we have more effective instruments of propaganda and instruction than were possessed by our ancestors; but, second, that man's life-span is three-score years and ten, that we find it hard to change the thought-patterns formed in our childhood, and that all governments are at present engaged in implanting nationalistic thought-patterns in the minds of their subjects, young and old alike. As soon as we and our rulers desire it, modern methods of propaganda can be used to effect a change of thought-patterns within a single lifetime. Meanwhile nationalistic idolatry is likely to remain the religion for which men will lay down their lives in wars which, but for that religion, would never have been declared.

On the ideological level, the best antidote to nationalistic idolatry is a monotheism with its corollary (since God's fatherhood implies men's brotherhood) of mono-anthropism. At present we have pentakosiotheism and as many varieties of mutually hostile humans as there are of Heinz's soups and pickles. That any system of monotheism will come, in the near future, to be generally accepted seems very unlikely. But it should not be impossible to secure the wide and immediate acceptance of a form of what may be called cosmic ethics; and this, perhaps, might serve as a basis for a future monotheism. At present men think and act as though they had no duties towards Nature. The Catholic Church, for example, officially teaches that sub-human lives may be treated as though they were things. But to any realistic observer it is surely obvious that not only do we have no right to treat living beings as things; we have no right to treat even things as mere things. Things must be treated as though they were parts of a complex and beautifully co-ordinated living organism. We are beginning to discover that to treat them in any other way may be to condemn the whole human experiment to failure. The Golden Rule is to be applied to animate and inanimate Nature as well as to our fellow men. Treat Nature with charity and understanding, and Nature will repay you with unfailing gifts. Treat Nature aggressively, with greed and violence and incomprehension: wounded Nature will turn and destroy you. Theoretically, at least, the ancients understood these truths better than ourselves. The Greeks, for example, knew very well that hubris against the essentially divine order of Nature would be followed by its appropriate nemesis. The Chinese taught that the Tao, or indwelling Logos, was present on every level from the physical and the biological up to the spiritual; and they knew that outrages against Tao, in Nature no less than in man, would lead to fatal results. We have to recapture some of this old lost wisdom. If we fail to do this—if, presumptuously imagining that we can 'conquer' Nature, we continue to live on our planet like a swarm of destructive parasites—we condemn ourselves and our children to misery and deepening squalor and the despair that finds expression in the frenzies of collective violence.